BAD CODE

OVERCOMING BAD MENTAL CODE THAT SABOTAGES YOUR LIFE

DEBORAH JOHNSON

DJWorksMusic.com
Los Angeles

BAD CODE
OVERCOMING BAD MENTAL CODE THAT SABOTAGES YOUR LIFE

Copyright ©2016 Deborah Johnson

Johnson, Deborah, author

Issued in print and electronic format
ISBN 978-0-9885879-5-3 Hardbound
ISBN 978-0-9885879-4-6 Paperback
ISBN 978-0-9885879-6-0 eBook

*Because of the dynamic nature of the Internet, any web addresses or links con-
tained in this book may have changed since publication and may no
longer be valid.*

*Cover art by Vikiana, ©Deborah Johnson • Royalty free photos
Drawings by applemoment, ©Deborah Johnson • Commercial permission
Back cover photo by Jessica Johnson: www.JessicaJohnsonPhotography.net*

Visit Deborah's websites at: GoalsForYourLife.com; DJWorksMusic.com

Dedicated to
Dr. Stephen Tracey
who lived every moment to the fullest
until his heavenly graduation.

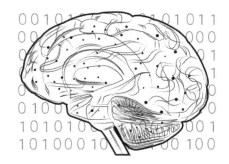

CONTENTS

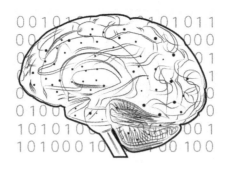

ACKOWLEDGEMENTS

Thank you to those who have generously allowed me to interview them: Robin Freeland, Aaron Copas, Austin Carson, Diana Hansen, Tage Peterson, Caryn Sawyer, Connie Pheiff, Dr. Stephen Tracey, Larry Beck, Dick Robertson, Nancy Graves, Maggie, Lynn Henish, Sid Malbon and Dr. Tony Coulson. I appreciate you all sharing a slice of your personal history with candidness and authenticity.

There is no way I could have embarked on a project like this without the keen eye of editors and readers. Many thanks to Paula Miller; a published author in her own right, who provided invaluable insight and guidance through the first drafts and structure of the book, followed by precise line-by-line editing in the final drafts. For many years she has trained college students, contributing to her ability to quickly ascertain not only grammatical errors but the quality and shape of a manuscript. Thank you to Sandra Grajeda with her unique clarity of concepts and lawyer's attention to detail. Her love of good poetry encourages creativity and her source-checking is beneficial to both readers and myself. I love and appreciate you both! Finally, my husband, Greg, my confidante and love of my life. You patiently listened through first drafts of concepts and questions during our morning coffees, picked and arranged amazing rose bouquets from our garden and lifted my spirits with your unique insight and humor. His thoroughness with the concepts and applications for each tool pushed me to make sure the meat of the book provided not only sound nutrition, but entertainment.

I have a couple small groups of amazing women I meet with periodically that create an invaluable sounding board and support team in my life. A special thank you to Peggy, Marcia, Jamie, Jo Anne and Dianne for making me take a break now and then for fun adventures and praying me through my many projects!

I won the lottery with my parents. They have provided guidance and love throughout my life, which I don't take for granted as I know many who have not been as fortunate. They instilled in me the tools of positive mental code that have helped me climb through more than a few obstacles that have come my way. That healthy code has also provided me with the personal tools to give to others without a tremendous amount of baggage.

Lastly, I'd like to thank my three sons Mike, Dan and David. They are all amazing in their own unique way and it's a joy to see them carve their paths in life. My role as a mom has changed to "watching the journey" and it is fun to see them grow and learn as they embark upon their future decades of life. I love you all! My talented and dear daughter-in-law took my photo—I love you Jessica! And what can I say about little Harper, other than after years of being surrounded by testosterone and smelly socks, having a bit of pink in my life is absolutely delightful! Yes, I'm the luckiest woman alive with the gift of my family and dear friends.

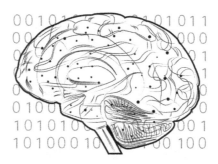

INTRODUCTION

Bad code brings discontentment based on shame and self-doubt, which is ultimately destructive- you'll never be good enough, so why try?

It felt like hundreds of hours had gone by while I watched a spinning circle on my computer screen. My edited web pages were not loading and I knew there was a deeper problem lurking under the guise of a possible Internet or server problem. I was right.

I knew very little about computer code, but through numerous searches, blogs and letting my nerdy side dive, unrestrained into research, I discovered the problem. I had contracted a bad code. A virus had infected every page of my website. As I worked to correct the problem, I contemplated the implications of "bad codes" and how malicious messages not only corrupt our computers but our own thinking and decision making as well. Thus, the idea of bad code versus good code was conceived, consequently instigating this book.

The Web of Code
While struggling to restore my website, I made a trip to Costco, where I couldn't help but pick up a copy of E.B. White's *Charlotte's Web*.[1] The endearing story about Wilbur the pig and his best friend Charlotte, an enterprising and creative spider, is one of my favorites. Revisiting the book reminded me that children's books aren't just for children. They are also for adults.

To my surprise, I found that Charlotte infused her web with "good code" to create a lifesaving message for her friend Wilbur, whose destiny was to be pork roast for the farmer's dinner. As Charlotte spun the words "SOME PIG" into her glistening web, her message created quite a stir among the whole town, which bought her good friend more time and ultimately, protection. The wise spider knew how to create positivity with positive talk.

Good code, just like the words woven in Charlotte's web, is positive, forward thinking and healthy. It doesn't always tell someone she is wonderful or "TERRIFIC," like Charlotte's second message. However, elevating a person or event is constructive and strategically beneficial in many ways.

Negative Code

In contrast, negative code seeps in our thoughts to discourage us, to tell us we're not good enough, messaging you that we need to be better or different to be accepted by others. It tells us we're too old, too fat, too dumb. These kinds of mental missives hinder both our personal and professional growth. Bad code brings discontentment based on shame and self-doubt, which is ultimately destructive. It tells us we'll never be good enough, so why try?

Bad code affects our personal lives, including our core being, our personality, goals, dreams, family and health. Bad code also affects our professional lives. Negativity often brings bitterness, anger and resentment and paralysis. Since our personal and professional lives intersect in many ways, it's important to consider both. As I further explored "bad code," I remembered another incident.

I Can Change This Dream

Some years ago, I was in a small village in a third-world country. The tiny house with multiple bedrooms and had a small, shallow pool out front. Getting to the front door required going around the pool or through the water to enter. Inside, the boxlike rooms were small but adequate. My family and I were figuring out room assignments when we heard news of a terrorist threat.

Entire towns were being annihilated around us. We faced serious danger. We were told to be extremely careful coming and going. I needed to go on an errand, so I was watchful, looking all around the property as I made my way to a car, which was out front. The vehicle, an older model, had a long front seat made of powder blue leather, something like our grandparents used to drive with a floorboard hump in the middle, wide enough for three to four people to sit across comfortably.

From the front seat, I saw a little yellow bus just a few yards away, the kind that transports kids to school. My husband boarded the bus with another gentleman. I watched as they entered.

Then, a rickety bus with chipped white paint and blackened windows slowly pulled up. My stomach turned with nausea from dread and fear. My shortened breaths turned to gasps. I was afraid, not only for myself, but also for my family.

When I saw two men emerge through the grimey bus door wearing what looked like white spacesuits, gas masks and holding rifles, my fears were confirmed. I wanted to scream, "Watch out!" to my husband and others in their small yellow bus, but there was no time. Frozen in fear, I sank to my knees, then ducked low to the floorboard and prayed. If this was to be the end, I was hoping to pass out first.

I knew I'd be dead in a matter of minutes then I realized, "That was a dream! I can change that dream!" With that, I decided my family would survive with a different outcome. Half-dazed and foggy brained, I awakened and stumbled out of bed.

Walking Away

I walked away from my dream, or nightmare, with insight. So many people suffer through lives stuck in a cycle of bad dreams, negativity, and bad codes. They have created worlds with seemingly no escape, cowering down on car floorboards. Swathed in dread, they can't wake up, fearing they'll be dead in minutes.

In the midst of my terrifying dream, I chose to wake up. It was an active decision because I didn't want my family or myself to die like helpless victims. If I had let the dream run it's full course, I have no idea of what the outcome would be. I can only imagine I might have started screaming to wake up my entire household, or worse, suffered a massive heart attack.

My dream was intensely realistic and dramatic. The vividness of the colors and action drew me in, and the fact that I could recall every detail so well made it even more believable and worthy of sharing. It also confirmed my belief that if I can change my dream, I can change my life. The same is true for you.

Beautiful and Astonishing

Bad code affects every area of your life by corrupting your view of good health, legitimate success, wise financial decisions, and your personal worth. How do you deal with that bad code? Do you erase it? Do you change it? Do you revise it? How can you lessen its power over you?

What would happen in your life if you could change bad mental code into good mental code? This book was conceived because I had a direct run-in with bad code on my computer, a children's book, and a terrifying dream. I found there are many principles in virtual and imaginary worlds that apply to the physical world.

Charlotte's end message to Wilbur was, "We're born, we live a little while, we die. By helping you, [Wilbur], perhaps I was trying to lift up my life a trifle. Heaven knows anyone's life can stand a little of that."[2] Charlotte had fulfilled her purpose completely and communicated to her friend that life is beautiful
and astonishing, as well as heartbreaking. How you lift up your life will make a difference in how it turns out for you.

Associating those great life principles with real-life applications is the goal of this book. Each chapter will give you the tools to not only change bad code into good code, but also defend yourself against fiery darts that have stabbed you throughout the decades of your life. When your dream, or nightmare becomes so vivid that you find yourself crouched in terror, you will have the power to wake up, change your dream, and change your life.

If you can change your dream, you can change your life.

I have included some interviews of ordinary people with extraordinary insights in the last section of this book. With unflinching candor they share their stories as portraits of their eras. I hope their stories will inspire you and help you. My desire is for you to look at life with good and healthy code that is beautiful, astonishing, and inspiring so that you can truly fulfill your purpose, even changing some of your bad dreams to good ones. Here's to cleaning up bad code, replacing it with good code, and freeing up your life!

PART ONE

TYPES OF CODE

The Essence of
Good and Bad Code

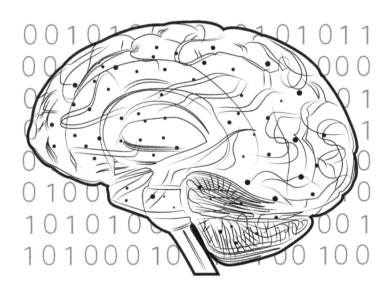

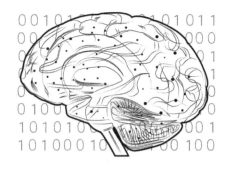

CHAPTER 1

CODE OF REASON: DEFINITION

Different types of code play a role in your everyday life. How you define it, use it and limit it will determine much of your future.

The actual definition of code is a "system of letters, numbers or symbols that gives information about something." It is a method by which normal language is converted to allow information to be communicated secretly, briefly or electronically. When applied to a computer, it is a system of symbols, numbers or signals that conveys information. The first known use of the Latin word was in the fourteenth century,[1] making code a principle that has continued throughout history.

To reason is to "identify your aim, your goal or your purpose." Some type of code helps you decipher your reason. Your brain deciphers some manner of code every time you hear someone speak or send a verbal or written message. Different types of code play a role in your everyday life. How you define it, use it and limit it will determine much of your future. Understanding mental code also gives you the power to change your thoughts and dreams of the future.

Recurring Bad Code

When I encountered the bad code of a website virus, the spinning circle on my computer resembled the spinning habitual mental cycle so many confront. It was similar to a continuous hamster wheel: a vicious circle of despair, heartbreak, anger and resentment. Just as the inability to eliminate bad code disabled my computer and kept it from functioning, I realized our own human codes and thought processes can keep many of us from making positive changes or developing new habits to move forward in life and achieve new goals.

Rewriting and replacing corrupted code takes time. While attempting to fix and delete some of the corrupted code on my web pages, I encountered additional problems. I panicked when my website completely disappeared during one of my experiments. To find a solution, I sought professional help. The permanent solution, I learned, involved throwing away any source file containing the bad code, which included much of my website theme. Unless all the bad code on my website was completely erased, the code would keep recurring and multiplying, replicating just like a physical virus.

How often do the same problems rear their head over and over in your life, spinning and spreading just like that virus, creating emotional bankruptcy? Issues caused by bad mental code will spread havoc and will never go away, unless you get to the source of the problem. Some examples are: weight, life focus, fear of the future, toxic relationships and poor life management.

Breaking Free

Just like experiencing, then waking up from a vivid nightmare, you can be crouched and clutching the floorboard of life with everything blowing up around you. Or you can choose to wake up, walk away, break free and change your life's picture and situation. No one's life is perfect and there are many who are struggling with extremely difficult circumstances. However, you have the choice and power to change your attitudeand even your situation with the small steps of first waking up to the reality of your situation. After that realization, you can implement the action it takes to create good mental code.

You can live with satisfaction, contentment and joy that infuses your decisions about health, relationships and business. You have the power to break free from a recurring nightmare and change bad mental code to good mental code. The bullets may still be flying, but they don't have to corrupt your dream. Why? Because you can change your dream by changing your code!

You have the power to break free from a recurring nightmare and change bad mental code to good mental code.

What is Healthy Fear?

Some feeling of fear and discontent is a good sign. That state of restlessness can motivate us to change. For example, consider the American Revolution. If our founding fathers were not content with the way the British were treating them, the Boston Tea Party would not have transpired. Paul Revere would have never taken his famous ride, risking his life not only with the ride, but crossing the sea in the midst of great opposition. We would never have the freedoms we enjoy in America today without their discontent and maybe a few nightmares thrown in along the way.

The same kind of discontent drives some professional athletes. Kobe Bryant would never have achieved his stardom without some discontent in the sharpness of one or more of his skills, prodding him to keep up a rigorous practice schedule. Jason Kendall would have never been named all-star catcher and achieved his hitting average by merely depending on his previous knowledge of baseball. In fact, Jason realized by improving his skills as a catcher, he would increase his chances at competing in the major leagues.[2]

Is Discontent the Enemy?

In pursuing change, consider the motive. Why are you discontent? Is it for the right reasons? Contentment is described as a state of "satisfaction and peacefulness." That is where most want to be, but to find such satisfaction may bring precarious times of discontentment, along with the willingness to work hard. How many people say they've found happiness? The answers vary. For instance, the HPI (Happy Planet Index) gives the United States a score of 37.3 percent. In fact, the U.S. is ranked 105 out of 151 of all the countries analyzed. The HPI is calculated on well-being, life expectancy and ecological footprint.[3]

The Gallup poll number for the U.S. is different at about 70%, evaluated on property, health, someone to count on, generosity, freedom to make life choices and freedom from corruption.[4] So if the U.S. overall happiness is so high, why do the books on finding happiness and self-improvement jump off the shelves every January? Top releases on Amazon in January 2016 were on grit, goals and resiliency, suggesting many people are looking for meaning and satisfaction, especially at the start of a new year.

Happiness Levels

Arthur Stone, a professor of psychiatry at Sony Brook University in New York, tracked the emotions of nearly 350,000 Americans and found that short-term happiness peaks at age twenty, dips in midlife, and then peaks again around age seventy. Why? One of the big theories is that when you're younger, you look ahead for what you're hoping to achieve in life. When you get older, you know where you are in life and start focusing on smaller matters like friends, families or hobbies.[5]

This interesting "U-shaped" dip for the middle decades is where life tends to be a busy scramble with growing families and aging parents. It's a logical assumption that stress levels are higher in those dipped years, thus the happiness and satisfaction levels go down until life evens out.[6] The tools you develop now will help you weather the rise and fall of happiness as well as stress, no matter what decade you're in. You don't have to stay in a spinning stupor, like that ever turning computer icon, hopeful for some new remedy. Unhealthy fear freezes you in a crouched position, where you hope to pass out before you no longer can move. You may not realize you can wake yourself up with the power and intelligence that is within you.

Fluid and Crystallized Intelligence

Many brain researchers divide intelligence into two categories; *fluid* and *crystallized* intelligence. Fluid intelligence is your ability to solve new problems. It appears effortless as it's based on your raw intelligence and shines as natural talent. Your genes play a part in fluid intelligence. For instance, if one of your children suddenly appears to have a natural athletic or musical ability, you may be able to trace it back to a previous generation.

Crystallized intelligence can grow and stretch throughout your life.

Crystallized intelligence is learned throughout your life. This type of intelligence can continue to grow and stretch for many all throughout their life. Chess and game show champions have developed their crystalized intelligence, even in the later decades of life.[7] You can do the same.

MINDSETS:

• Remember, you have the power to change your dream and transform bad mental code to healthy good mental code with new habits and positive self-talk.

• Use fear and lack of contentment to fight complacency, unhealthy contentment, apathy or indifference.

• Focus on crystallized intelligence to continue to learning and growing throughout your whole life, no matter what age.

• Maintain your own healthy mindset to break free from a recurring nightmare and change bad mental code to good mental code.

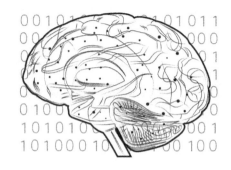

CHAPTER 2

CODE OF EFFECTIVENESS: MORSE CODE

Morse Code is a good example of how a basic and simple solution can hold the most effective resolution.

Changing your dream involves the active decision of waking up in order to change bad code to good code. After identification of your recurring nightmare, you must resolve to change. The same arousing principle applies to setting and achieving goals. To change bad mental code to good mental code, you need to wake up to the fact that you are being sabotaged by bad code. At this point you may realize you need to change it. However, how do you change it and to what?

Code has become more sophisticated through time as a necessary part of international society. In fact, the advancement of civilization has relied on code. The evolution of these codes also reveals the way bad and good mental code affect you in your daily life. The first is the somewhat simple, yet effective Morse Code. Its invention had a profound impact on modern life.

International Language

Glenn Pladsen told the story of how Morse code saved the Navy Destroyer, USS Wood in 1973, when all power was out. Pladsen had joined the Navy as a Cryptology Technician, which supports the national intelligence gathering effort with an emphasis on codes. Learning Morse code was part of his training. When the large destroyer lost all communication due to the failure of generators, they were stranded in shipping lanes, not able to move in the pitch dark of night.

Soon, there was a large freighter headed straight for them. The enterprising crew had to think quickly. Since Morse code is an international language, they were able to signal a Russian destroyer that was fairly close by. The destroyer saw the flashes of light, which were sent on battery powered flashing lanterns, signaling an S-O-S distress message.

S-O-S

The Russian destroyer diverted the freighter headed directly for the USS Wood and stayed with the USS Wood until power was regained.[1] The simple and effective S-O-S signal was what prevented a huge and devastating collision for the USS Wood that would have killed many aboard. S-O-S is not an acronym for any particular word, but the letters were chosen because they are easy to transmit in Morse code.

Morse code has been a system used with much success for decades, especially in military operations. Invented by Samuel F.B. Morse, Joseph Henry and Alfred Vail, it is a series of long and short sounds and light flashes used to symbolize the content of a message. Morse code has been used for over 160 years—longer than any other electrical coding system. The simplicity of the transmission of Morse code for the USS Wood made it vital and effective in averting a huge tragedy.

In times where entire networks can go down with a power outage or natural disaster, Morse code, less sensitive to poor signal conditions, can be comprehensible without a decoding device. Three dots, three dashes, then three dots of S-O-S continues to save lives.

The Information Age

Morse code signaled the beginning of the information age. Samuel Morse also invented the single-circuit telegraph, which revolutionized long-distance communication between nations. Before this, some nations used smoke signals and drumbeats to exchange information.

Morse code was transmitted across telegraph wires. Even though the code assigned letters in the alphabet and numbers as a set of dots and dashes, based on the frequency of use, some letters were simplified and operators were soon able to understand the code by just listening to the click of the receiver.

Dits and Dahs and spaces give a characteristic sound to each of the thirty-six letters. Each letter has a different sound, beat and rhythm. Operators must send the complete sound with the correct rhythm to communicate effectively. The spacing between the letters is extremely important and can make a huge difference between the meaning of the message.

The Rhythm of Morse Code

If you hear the sounds dit-dah-dit-dit (space) dah-dah-dah (space) dit-dah-dah, the word is L-O-W. If you hear the same sounds, but different spacing, such as dit (space) dah-dit (space) dit (space) dah-dah (space) dah-dit-dah-dah, the word translates as E-N-E-M-Y. This is all because of the spacing of the sounds, even though they are in the same order.[2]

Spacing between words should be a little longer and can get tricky, taking more work to master. It casts a whole new light on the meaning of "smooth operator," for with good technique, the message will come across clearly and effectively.

Many people struggle with basic effective communication skills. This often comes up in business, partnerships or in marriage. Varying backgrounds, lack of verbal skills, cultural differences and deficiency of commitment all contribute to a discordant cacophony. Clear and effective communication is very important in building strong relationships. If there is misunderstanding or an impending collision of opinions and views, returning to a basic message and method can improve the situation.

Physical Effectiveness
Just as the correct tools and techniques are important in Morse code for effective communication, there are effective ways to verbally and physically communicate, whether with a friend, spouse or colleague. A harsh tone, a drawn out word or an angry look all communicate something different, even if the actual word and message is "love." For example, an EMT's calm tone of voice helps an anxious person relax when faced with an emergency.

A sincere smile, look or "I love you" transmits a simple physical message of devotion and even at times, commitment. A head-nod or thumbs-up will encourage a speaker or friend to continue on the same path. Those are simple, easy, timeless and effective signals, just as uncomplicated as the Morse code.

Small acts of kindness and encouragement that are uncomplicated and unexpected are welcome components in a world that seems at times, disposable and harsh.

Morse code will always remain a viable way of providing communication that is reliable during difficult conditions. In the same way, small acts of kindness and encouragement that are uncomplicated and unexpected are welcome components in a world that seems at times, disposable and harsh.

Upgraded Code

Experienced Morse code operators can easily converse at twenty to thirty words a minute. Morse code was even upgraded in 2003 to include the @ symbol, often used in email addresses, as the first change to the system since before World War II.[3] It is interesting that there is no exclamation point, which makes the accuracy of the message even more crucial.

The upgrade, ironically, allows ham radio operators to exchange emails more easily. When Morse died in 1972, more than 650,000 miles of telegraph wire circled the globe. By early twentieth century, messages were sent wirelessly. The world had forever changed.

The sophistication of code and communication has plodded stubbornly, then multiplied persistently to where we are today. If people would take it upon themselves to augment their personal communication skills, messages would be clearer, better-received and constructive. Morse Code is a good example of how a basic and simple solution can hold the most effective resolution, just as in diverting a Russian destroyer.

To change bad mental code to good mental code, you need to wake up to the fact that you are being sabotaged by bad code.

 MINDSETS:

• Embrace the fact that code has become more sophisticated, but a necessary part of international society.

• Review some of the effective ways to verbally and physically communicate with simple tools illustrated by Morse Code, whether with a friend, spouse or colleague. Examples are tone of voice, eye contact and kind words.

• Take it upon yourself to augment your personal communication skills. Your messages will be more uncomplicated, better-received and constructive.

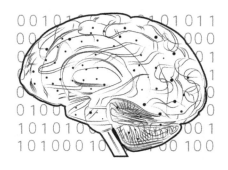

CHAPTER 3

CODE OF IDENTIFICATION: UPC

You have a distinct personal identity, or personal trade number that is different than anyone else's.

Another simple, yet effective code is the UPC, or Universal Product Code. It is not relayed by sound or flashes of light, but by numbers. The first item marked with a UPC scanned at a retail checkout was at the Marsh supermarket in Troy, Ohio in 1974. The item of purchase was all of sixty-seven cents for a ten-pack of Wrigley's Juicy Fruit chewing gum.[1]

The UPC is a symbol of lines and numbers placed on products that are scanned during point of sale. The UPC not only identifies the product, but contains product information. All carry unique codes with the same purpose, which is identification. A UPC code illustrates the importance of a personal identity as yours is different than anyone else's on the planet.

Identify and Inform

UPC's are used on most pieces of merchandise you see today. Some of the codes are different lengths and in different formats, but they all serve the same purpose, which is to identify and inform.

The number you see underneath the UPC barcode symbol is the Global Trade Item Number. Used in both the physical and the digital worlds, the GTINs identify products at retail point-of-sale and on items in a warehouse. Each company is assigned a six number prefix. I applied and received my UPC unique prefix a number of years ago from the Uniform Code Council and have used it on all my recorded products. A GTIN, along with a UPC is universal and can be used anywhere in the world.

Every different item, including different sizes of items, needs their own UPC. If you are not selling multiple products, or are working through a particular distributor you may not need your own trade number. However, just like a UPC code, you have a distinct personal identity, or personal individuality that is different than anyone else's. No one in the universe has your exact number, look or personality.

The brain's circuitry amplifies the complexity of electronic circuitry
with a tightly coiled road map of paths,
firing points and signals.

Decoder

The very last digit on the UPC is the check number. There is an exact formula to figure this out, with adding the even and odd numbers together. I have to admit at times, I've made my mistakes in calculating this figure using my personal UPC number! The bar code scanner will verify the exact product through the exactness of this number, so it is necessary to get it correct.

A barcode reader, or scanner is an electronic device that can read and output printed barcodes. It consists of a light source, a lens and a light sensor. You can readily see these in most supermarket checkout counters as well as other retail stores. Most all barcode readers contain decoder circuitry that changes a code into a set of signals. A decoder translates the code.

The opposite of decoding is encoding, as it creates the code. The "Television Decoder Circuitry Act of 1990" required television receivers with picture screens thirteen inches or larger to have built-in decoder circuitry designed to display closed captioned television transmissions for the deaf. The Federal Communications Commission also applied this requirement to computers equipped with television circuitry, sold with monitors larger than thirteen inches.[2] This fact may not seem currently relevant, but it demonstrates the importance of decoding in history, as pertaining to not only the deaf, but also for communication and information.

Your Number

Of all the different codes you process mentally, your identity is perhaps the most difficult to recognize, affirm and decode. However, it is the most vital to construct accurately as it serves as a foundation for creating good and healthy mental code. There is no way a UPC will identify your distinct character, but the fact that your DNA is different than everyone else's on the planet is worth acknowledging.

> *Of all the different codes you process mentally, your identity is perhaps the most difficult to recognize, affirm and decode.*

All you need to do is watch people for even ten minutes to see that every single person, as well as moving object, has a distinct identity. I'm a farm girl at the core, probably from my roots on a dairy farm in Georgia, and I love watching the birds in our yard. My husband has taken it upon himself to be the main birdfeeder. The endless variety and personalities of feathered friends that choose to perch on a tiny wobbly platform to obtain a few seeds never ceases to entertain us during our mornings, as we sip high-octane coffee.

Just as there are over ten thousand different varieties of birds and countless varieties of other species on the earth,[3] there are endless varieties of people, personalities, intelligence and ideas surrounding you on a daily basis. However, it's important to go a step further to characterize your identity. This is a contemplative component that haunts many throughout their lifetime. You discover who you are not only through what you do but through your thoughts, responses and brain circuitry. There are many elements to identify, but your responses are a good place to start. Do you shut down after one discouraging event, or are you able **to** keep firing emotionally and moving ahead? If you have competed at all, whether in sports, the arts or even writing or speaking, it is helpful to develop the quality of resilience to bounce back and keep your spirits up after unexpected outcomes.

There are many elements to identify, but your
responses are a good place to start.

The Decoding Brain

Decoding is a necessary part of identifying a UPC code. Decoding is related to circuitry, and everyone fires and responds to different inputs in their life. The brain is an amazing decoding mechanism. When you look at a rose, drawing it close to smell and touch it, millions of circuits fire in your brain to identify the look, smell, color and shape of the rose.

As complicated as electronic circuitry can be, the brain's circuitry amplifies the complexity with a tightly coiled road map of paths, firing points and signals. The complexity and power of the brain gives you the power to identify and change your mental code, becoming a powerful tool.

Your Circuits

If you have ever strung Christmas or patio lights, you may have experienced a bulb going out. With a *series* circuit, when one light goes out, all the lights go out. This proves very frustrating when you have finally finished stringing multiple sets of lights then realize an entire area is dark because of one light. The challenge lies in finding which light is out. I have often just thrown the whole string of lights away, as it's a frustrating time-waster to distinguish and change the faulty bulb without the correct tools.

In contrast, if your lights are on a *parallel* circuit, when a single light goes out, the other lights still glimmer and glow brightly. This begs the question, what type of circuitry is firing in your brain? Do you emotionally shut down if one experience doesn't go as planned or do you have the parallel focus to keep your mind from the tangled web of negativism and pessimism? Understanding your strengths along with forming realistic expectations assist in creating a parallel focus that is healthy mental code.

As you ponder your personal circuitry, whether series or parallel, it will help you decode your personal UPC and identity. Your identity is an important part of your life to consider as you travel through the decades of your life. Just as every product has a UPC code, every living object is identifiable with certain characteristics and qualities.

MINDSETS:

• Identify your distinct personal identity, or personal trade number that is different than anyone else. No one in the universe has your exact number, look or personality, just as every UPC code is different.

• Reflect on the complexity and power of the brain, as it gives you the power to identify and change your mental code. It will become a powerful tool in changing negativism and pessimism.

• Ponder your personal circuitry, whether series or parallel and what positive changes you can make. It will help you decode your personal UPC and identity.

• Create a parallel focus that will steer your mind away from negativism and pessimism.

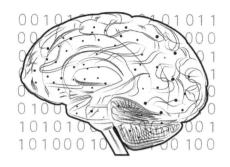

CHAPTER 4

CODE OF UNIQUENESS: ISRC

You have a unique ISRC internal stamp that is uniquely yours, different than anyone else that gives you your own digital fingerprint.

The ISRC, or International Standard Recording Code, is an addition to the UPC code with every CD, in that it identifies the specific parts of a recorded project. Each ISRC is a unique and permanent identifier for a particular recording or song. Only one ISRC is issued for each track, and an ISRC can never represent more than one unique recording. Just like the ISRC, you have qualities that uniquely identify you.

The ISRC code is assigned to songs and encoded into a compact disc for tracking purposes. (royalties, etc.) Each song has a unique code consisting of a series of twelve letters and numbers. The tracking code has expanded to include all types of sound and music video recordings.

Just like the ISRC, you have qualities that uniquely identify you.

AAD. ADD. DDD

In the past, many classical CD's had a three-letter code indicating the recording technology, such as AAD, ADD or DDD. "A" stands for analog, while "D" stands for digital. The third letter will always be D as the technology for transfer is digital. With the resurgence of analog recording and the popularity of vinyl records, you may see these symbols in some retro stores or estate sales.

ISRCs are widely used in digital commerce by downloading sites and collecting societies. They are a "digital fingerprint" that will show up to identify the recording. It is a unique, reliable and international identification system.

Your ISRC

You have a specific personal identity both in appearance and personality. In fact, each part is unique to just you, creating your own digital fingerprint. Your hair color, eyes, facial features, body type, personality and other characteristics distinguish you from every other person on the planet. Even twins, though they may look strikingly similar in physical appearance, will have some distinct quality if you examine them closely and get to know them.

For example, I attended high school with a set of identical twins, both dancers. They performed in many of the Disneyland parades and I envied their high kicks and flexibility as suppleness is not one of my strong physical attributes. Interestiingly, both twins were good athletes and upon first glance, looked completely identical. However, once I knew them individually, I recognized their distinct characteristics and personalities, thus I could tell them apart. This familiarity was very helpful in our friendship, as I am certain the girls grew tired of constantly being compared with each another.

Identical twins come from the same egg, fertilized by the same sperm, having the same DNA sequence. Environment plays a role in distinctness and is different in every situation. Also, even though heredity is a main factor, the environment also affects disease and susceptibility of life-changing illnesses, such as schizophrenia in twins.[1] Only fifty percent share the disease. This is an interesting fact not only for twins, but for the population as a whole. You may have many of the same internal components as other family members, but still be very unique in size, height, weight and personality. Your environment and choices create the distinct tapestry of your life beyond your genetic makeup.

Your Bones

At birth, you arrive with 270 bones in your body. This total decreases to 206 by adulthood as some bones fuse. Further, the male and female skeleton differ as the female is equipped for childbirth. To further that reasoning, each human skeleton supports distinctive body types as varied as shades in a rainbow. A rainbow has a continuous spectrum of shades with an infinite number of colors.

Part of your skeletal structure is the skull. The skull is a very complex structure and at birth is made up of forty-four separate bony elements. During development, many of those elements fuse and create facial features that are uniquely yours. Your identity may be comprised of many combinations, like being an Afro-American female of English descent, five-feet seven with brown eyes and shoulder-length hair.

Beyond that, you have a unique ISRC internal stamp that is uniquely yours, different than anyone else that gives you your own centrifugal force in this life. You don't need to apply tattoos all over your body to look unique, although that does add to an individual style. Your inner genetic stamp, or makeup, hormonal controls, diet and stress all play a part in your outer appearance.

19

Healthy Internal ISRC

Much of your healthy internal ISRC, or internal health is based on what you eat. Good eating habits depend on good choices. Eating a couple chocolates won't cause obesity, but super-sized portions, abundance of fried and fatty foods and diabetic tendencies will. In California, more than thirteen million adults (forty-six percent of all adults in the state) are estimated to have prediabetes—a precursor to type 2 diabetes—or undiagnosed diabetes.

An additional 2.5 million adults have diagnosed diabetes. That means fifty-five percent of all California adults have prediabetes or diabetes. That is staggering! In today's dollars, a person who is diagnosed with diabetes by age forty will have lifetime medical spending that is $124,600 more than someone who is not.[2]

Dr. Harold Goldstein, executive director of the Health Advocacy Center in Davis, California says,"For most people, type 2 diabetes is entirely preventable." However, merely throwing money into programs and regulating sugary drinks will not solve the problem. A focus on lifestyle and daily routine changes will.

Making constant good choices with moderation is the very best diet for maintaining your healthy internal codes.

One of our sons, Daniel Johnson, was a very successful personal trainer for a number of years before becoming an attorney. He says that sound nutrition, not fad diets, will get you to your goal quicker than anything else. Making constant good choices with moderation is the very best diet. Today, you have more choices than ever for your unique taste, preference and style. There is good and accurate feedback for your internal health if you seek it out, just as the ISRC code allows for music artists to receive feedback.

Accurate Feedback

With the number of different and unique recorded products available, the IRSC code allows music artists to receive accurate feedback and be paid. Without it, many performers and writers would have no means to survive financially.

Your relationships and experiences will help you understand and define your uniqueness and exclusive traits.

There are no specific IRSC codes for your health, as it merely serves to illustrate your uniqueness. However, the ability to process accurate, and hopefully constructive feedback from those in your life is vital to maintaining and developing good mental code that will pay off with internal satisfaction and peacefulness, which is a component of personal happiness. Your relationships and experiences will help you understand and define your uniqueness and exclusive traits beyond your genetic code.

 MINDSETS:

• Identify areas of your environment and personal choices that are influencing your characteristics beyond your genetic makeup, including hair color, eyes, facial features, body type and personality.
• Evaluate your diet choices, whether good or bad, to maintain your healthy internal code.
• Define the relationships and experiences that give you constructive feedback in order to maintain and develop good and healthy mental code.

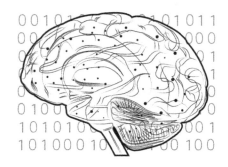

CHAPTER 5

CODE OF ORIGIN: BINARY

Reversing or changing the order of zeros and ones in binary code will change the meaning, demonstrating how reversing a mindset can change simple commands for your life.

Binary code is another simple code, consisting of a string of 0's and 1's. The basis for binary code was discovered by Gottfried Leibniz in 1679.[1] Presently, there is a string of binary code for each symbol, command or instruction on a computer, thus its importance. For example, a binary string of eight binary digits (bits) can represent any of 256 possible values, therefore corresponding to a variety of different instructions.

All computer language is based in binary code. It is the back end of all computer functioning. Computer functions will rapidly toggle between 00 or 01 at an incomprehensible speed, and this is how computers can assist humans. However, the human brain functions holistically at much more rapid speeds than a computer in doing other types of very complicated tasks.[2] The average person's brain contains over 100 billion neurons, or nerve cells. Binary code, as a very basic and specific code, is a good example of how important it is to be specific and exact in many areas of life.

Life Reduced to Numbers

Leibniz was trying to find a system that would confirm his theory that life could be simplified or reduced to straightforward propositions. Basically, binary simplifies information processing. It is the smallest numbering system that can be used, as there must always be at least two symbols for a processing system to work. As with many researchers, Leibniz's ideas and research was not readily accepted and adopted. However, its importance is verified in the technology we enjoy today because of it.

As with Morse code, binary code is simple in theory. However, one small change in spacing between the dits and dahs in Morse code will change an entire word or sentence. In the same way, reversing or changing the order of zeros and ones in binary code will change the meaning, demonstrating how reversing a mindset can change simple commands for your life. Code is very specific and that fact has not changed throughout history.

Bad Code Song

An illustration of a simple code that was misread happened when I wrote the fun and upbeat song "Bad Code" to help introduce this book.[3] After submitting the artwork and .wav sound file for digital downloads and the CD release, I got a message from the distributor. They had rejected my artwork, as it was in Greek and they wanted me to know it may not sell in all countries because of this.

I immediately went on their website and contacted the company. I asked the representative to look at the artwork, as the front cover contained the simple binary code of zeros and ones, not the Greek language. He immediately recognized the mistake, one probably made by a computer or assistant who had no idea what 00 and 01 meant. After rectifying the the problem, he approved the album. It was a simple fix for the misunderstanding of a simple code. This incidence shows that many times there are simple fixes for problems. In a similar way, your health habits can greatly affect your mental code. Like the simple change that cleared the confusion about my CD artwork, simple ways in the way we behave can have a profound effect on our outlook.

Basic Needs

Abraham Maslow in his 1943 paper "A Theory of Human Motivation"[4] defined the hierarchy of human needs with physiological needs providing the base of his pyramid. Air, food and water are metabolic requirements for survival in all animals, including humans.

There are four other items on top of the triangle including safety, love/belonging, esteem and self-actualization. Maslow emphasizes the onslaught of stress when there is a threat to the basics of the pyramid, which is breathing, eating and drinking. Even though Maslow's hierarchy has been questioned, he addressed many of the basic requirements for living that have been verified time and again. As a vital part of life in America, physical exercise fulfills a basic emotional as well as a physical need as it helps many to reduce their stress and minimize the effects of sedentary activities.

Exercise Code

On a recent morning at the gym, I was asked by an older gentleman on a stationary bike why I arrived at the gym so early every day. I quickly responded, "To get it done!" He then replied, "That's not a good enough answer!" I was taken aback as I've previously used that same response without question.

I thought for a moment then replied, "When I had three active sons four years and under, I started coming to the gym when it opened at five A.M. It was a great respite from the friendly hurricane at home. I still come that early, as it has become a habit and I gain the same results as when my kids were young. It relieves stress!"

You may not have three active sons four years and under, but you may have your own health issues, tough relationships, difficult business decisions or other concerns where sweating and working out hard will help you release stress and extract unhealthy toxins. There are many documented benefits to exercise and it's important to discover them and apply what works for you.

Birth of the Fitness Industry

The *Jack LaLanne Show* [5] made its debut in 1951 in the San Francisco, California area. It then went nationwide in 1959 with the simple props of a broomstick, chair and rubber cord, appealing to women nationwide. His show then ran until the mid-1980's. LaLanne became a national celebrity with his preaching regular exercise and proper diet. He basically started the fitness industry.

Robin Freeland started working as a trainer when the fitness industry began, at the time when Jack LaLane instigated his program. Robin was also competing as a bodybuilder and was doing quite well, with her amazing sculpted lean body mass and consistent strategy. However, she changed her emphasis when she saw so many competitors taking shortcuts using steroids. Robin decided to provide help and positive direction to others with a basic healthy approach to fitness by focusing on her work as an instructor, now helping others for four decades.

Most spend at least three hours daily doing those passive activities that are non work-related and sedentary in nature.

Robin defines some of the biggest obstacles people face in getting started in an exercise program, one being poor time management. She asks, "How many hours have you sat in front of your computer or watched a game or program in the past week?" Most spend at least three hours daily doing those passive activities that are non work-related and sedentary in nature.

Willingness to Change

To develop good and healthy mental code toward fitness, Robin Freeland says you need an open mind with a simple willingness to change. Sometimes that change is brought on because of a health issue that rouses you out of your personal procrastination from a refusal to see your true situation. It may also come when someone close to you experiences health problems and physical difficulties and you feel as if you just dodged a bullet because you remain in good health.

If you take little simple and basic steps to change habits and make small changes in diet and exercise, you will be more successful in gaining long term results. One thing that's certain, exercise doesn't just "happen." You usually have to plan for it. Just as binary code deals with merely zeros and ones, either you're in the chair or out of the chair. Get up out of the chair, off the couch, take the stairs or take a walk. Even if you don't belong to a gym, you can start moving. It is part of the mindset of creating good mental code and a healthier body.

Specific and exact go-to commands or actions give you a greater chance for successfully changing destructive thoughts to constructive thoughts. Simple commands are especially valuable when faced with a barrage of confusion and negative self-talk.

MINDSETS:

• Define a mindset you can reverse that will change a harmful command of your life, similar to changing the order of zeros and ones in binary code. An example is reversing a predetermined negative opinion to a disposition of openess.

• Note the hours of passive activities included in your day and what changes you can make to include more active activities and better physical health.

• Define some simple commands you can use when faced with a barrage of confusion and negative self-talk.

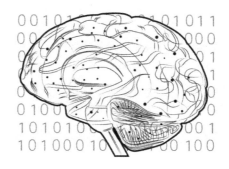

CHAPTER 6

CODE OF TOUCH: BRAILLE

Nonverbal ways of communicating support are much more powerful than the collective power of a Twitter feed, demonstrating the effectiveness of the code of touch.

Some code is felt and not seen, like Braille, a type of binary code for blind people to read and write. Braille is binary because each dot has two states: raised or not raised, making it binary in nature. The main braille cell has six dots consisting of three rows of two. With a compact system as this the fingers can easily move from one letter or symbol to the next.

Early attempts using a "felt" code for the blind used regular alphabet letters in raised print. Naturally that approach would seem easier to use than learning a whole new system. However, those raised print letters first tried in the early 1800's were very difficult to read merely by touching and the raised script proved even more difficult to write.

The Braille system of today was invented in the nineteenth century by Luis Braille, who completely lost his eyesight in a childhood accident. Braille's system was officially adopted in Amsterdam in 1854, two years after his death, but it did not come into wide use until 1916 in the United States.[1]

Reading and Writing

Braille has transformed the ability of the blind to successfully read with a simple but versatile method of touch-based reading and writing. There is a braille code for every foreign language imaginable and there are also braille codes for mathematics, music and computers, which is far-reaching as the system has opened doors of observation and work for many.

Braille is a good example of how important touch is in our society and within human relationships. The definition of touch is to make direct "contact." It is one of our five basic senses.

Dynamic Code

Dynamic is characterized by constant change, activity or progress. The type of message and method of contact changes with each occurence, thus it is dynamic in nature. Touch in human relationships is an incredible source of dynamic code. It communicates a vast range of feelings from love to hate, from security to anxiety, from trust to fear. Support from trusted connections increases your ability to create lasting change and transformation in your life with accountability, focus and encouragement.

The focus on narcissism and self-absorption is a subject
that will greatly affect future generations.

In the book *Generation Me,* Jean Twenge, Ph.D. says, "Today's young people speak the language of the self as their native tongue. The individual has always come first, and feeling good about yourself has always been a primary virtue."[2] To take this statement further, the present cultural focus on narcissism and self-absorption is a movement that will greatly affect future generations.

With social media, including Facebook, E-mail, YouTube, texts and Tweets, individuals feel a false sense of connectedness to others. With so many people sending text messages and receiving immediate responses, they may feel like they're part of a community, a fellow citizen among a sea of friends. However, an attachment to social media connections creates a false sense of reality. This illusion of "connectedness" is something like visiting a movie set. You can picture how a real a set looks, front and back. As you walk along the set, it looks realistic and inviting. For example, sitting on the sofas and chairs you see in the living room tempt you to sit and relax. However, if you walk behind that set door, you will often find the inviting scene is only pretend. Behind the scenes are boards and even junk that prop up the front of the facade. This frailty cannot be seen unless one explores the set from different angles.

In the same way, adding someone as your "friend" on social media doesn't let you see what's behind the façade of their posts. True friendships develop from seeing others face to face and then "accepting" the entire person, not just the glossy appearance from a Facebook profile. When you connect on a personal level, you recognize and acknowledge all the person's junk that lies behind the frontage.

Need to Belong

Because Millennials frequently change jobs, locations, social groups and interests, it is becoming more and more difficult for them to develop the same lifelong connections and bonds with a specific group, unlike the connections of generations past. In fact, older generations, despite the hardships and wars they experienced, knew they could count on each other. From the WWII Generation to Generation X, these social groups made lifelong friends and developed strong connections to their work colleagues. That's why survivors often experience depression, when those loyal comrades leave this world. Their empty spot is not easily filled.

Psychologists Baumeister and Leary state that the need to belong has two main features: frequent personal contacts or interactions with the other person, mostly pleasant; and the perception that there is an interpersonal bond or relationship marked by stability, concern and continuation into the foreseeable future.[3]

Most Facebook and social media friendships would not fit in that category. Posting, responding and communicating in solitude does not build close relationships. Currently, you can like, love, laugh, wow, be sad or angry in response to a post; those are all quick and at times, superficial ways of communicating.

Online Coolness

I love the lyrics to "Online" by Brad Paisley. The song contrasts illusion and reality: Online, our guy is mysterious, a black belt, drives a Maserati, lives in Malibu and is a 6'5" professional model. In reality, he lives at home, is overweight at 5'3", is still on *MySpace* and plays the tuba.[4]

The whole point of the song is that a person can be anyone he wants to be online. In fact, the singer is so much cooler online and wants to stay there. It would be a daunting and risky prospect for this kind of person to ever leave his parent's basement bedroom and reveal his authentic self.

To "be real" is to touch people. Remember those finger paintings you crafted while in primary grades; slopping dollops of paint on one side of a page, pressed together with the other side, creating a unique amalgamation of color? That mixture of hues is what happens when people touch each other. There is a little part of the color and blend that rubs off. Such a mingling is not achieved any other way.

The mixture of hues is what happens when people touch each other. There
is a little part of the color and blend that rubs off,
not achieved any other way.

Survival Rate

The benefit of having good connections with others cannot be ignored. Researchers analyzed 308,849 participants in 148 studies to find there was a fifty percent increased likelihood of survival for participants with strong social relationships. This finding was consistent across age, sex, health status and cause of death.[5] In fact, going further, they stated that lack of social relationships bring about the same risk factors as smoking and alcohol abuse and exceed the negative influence compared to other factors such as physical inactivity and obesity.

Those findings are fairly sobering, considering the growing disengagement in the present generation with a world that seems to be connected with tweets, pings and beeps, but is really divided and detached from others due to self-absorption. This isolating precipice is so steep that it surely holds many dangers in the years ahead if there are no modifications and alteration to young people's dependence on messaging that doesn't always communicate authentically and effectively.

Nonverbal Messages

Research on interpersonal attraction suggests that ninety-three percent of the meaning or impact of communication is transferred nonverbally.[6] Few challenge the basic concept that nonverbal communication is an extremely valuable form of communication.

With social media, you can't see the other person look away, (unless of course you are on a videocam!), roll their eyes or avoid direct eye contact. If you have had someone walk away from you while you are speaking, you understand how painful that action feels and the meaning of rejection or conflict it conveys. Those are all messages that can't be adequately communicated with a thumbs up or a "like" on social media.

Support from trusted connections increases your ability to create lasting change with accountability, focus and encouragement.

Even Morse code, with no symbol for an exclamation mark, is not able to sufficiently communicate a message with over-the top excitement or anger. If you have felt the calming effect of rubbing a baby's back, the touch of a friend's hand during a fearful time, the reassuring look from an audience when walking on a stage, you understand the power of nonverbal communication; all nonverbal gestures or expressions communicate a more powerful message or emotion than the collective power of any Twitter feed. It's vital to understand how important the code of touch and nonverbal messages are in our world today.

MINDSETS:

• Identify how you can use touch to communicate a vast range of emotion from love to hate, security to anxiety and trust to fear aside from social media.

• What false sense of connectness do you feel with social media, including Facebook, E-mail, YouTube, texts and Tweets?

• Identify two areas you feel the need to belong with a personal connection including touch. Next, name the interpersonal connections you have in your life to create stability, concern and continuation in those areas you have identified.

• Rate your level or lack of social relationships. Realize the lack of personal and authentic relationships brings health risks as serious as smoking, alcohol abuse, physical inactivity and obesity.

• Pursue those connections that will add healthy mental and resulting physical code to your life with a genuine touch, especially if you are starting to feel the repercussions of health risks listed above.

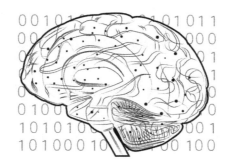

CHAPTER 7

CODE OF COMMUNICATION: SHORT CODE

*Too many short codes in life leave you with a concoction of wires
that may never meet and fire without a good plan
and method of action.*

In the 1940's the first recognizably modern electrically powered computers were created, many so large they filled the entire floor of a building. With limited speed and capacity, hand-written programs were generated with great effort.

In 1949, the language *Short Code* appeared for electronic devices and it required the human programmer to change its statements into 0's and 1's by hand. (Remember binary code?) It was the first step toward the complex computer languages of today, but took a great deal of time.[1]

In 1951, a computer program was written to turn the language's statements into 0's and 1's. This led to faster programming and meant the programmer no longer had to do the work by hand. The computer's brain now was functioning more on its own, translating messages instantly. There are many short code examples in life including finances, personal projects and brain stimulation; however, without accuracy of planning, time commitment and effort, disaster could be a click away.

Coding Errors

The human brain inherently performs much quicker than a computer. We understand how such programming works at the moment when a familiar friend or spouse completes your sentences or quickly responds to your comments. Their intrusions may seem bizarre at times, as if they can read minds. You are experiencing a form of short code. However, this form of short code, or completion, makes communication fast and immediately understood even with a shortened message.

If you are on the WordPress website platform, as many of us entrepreneurial types are, the WordPress-specific shortcode lets you do nifty things with very little effort. For instance, you can embed videos, TED Talks, audio files, images and documents. If I have worked on YouTube and want to embed a video on my web page, I will copy the embedded link, right beside the share link. I do have to place this link in the source code of the page, but it is very quick and easy to do.

Google has made it easier than ever for reluctant techies like me to edit and update their websites with this tool. However, if even one wrong symbol is placed in the code, the whole link will not work correctly. In fact, extra care must be taken for accuracy in using short codes. A message that is abbreviated incorrectly with an unclear meaning sent instantly across the Internet cosmos, can't be salvaged with any ease and may bring an unintended negative outcome. Verbal speech acts the same way. Every person has said something that brings immediate regret as they wish they could take back the hurtful comment or hasty rebuke. Words, spoken in haste have a corrupting influence, just like a coding error.

A message that is abbreviated incorrectly with an unclear meaning can't be salvaged with any ease of effort and may bring an unintended outcome.

Just as completing a good friend's sentences enhances a feeling of familiarity, shortcuts have made the creation of computer code easier. Likewise, there are new products out every day to help save time, money, energy and space. However, caution should be taken in using too many shortcuts, as the mess may be more difficult to rectify in the long run when errors occur. Financial principles act as a great illustration of shortcodes, especially when balancing a budget.

Don't Underfill the Jacuzzi

Have you ever under-filled the water level in a Jacuzzi tub? If you have, you know what happens when you turn on the jets. Water shoots out of control all across the room, getting not only you, but the room all wet as well. This same principle applies to finances if you don't wisely manage, save and plan ahead. The out of control spraying will create a huge mess, and you may even end up under water.

Money issues can cause a great deal of stress. The average U.S. household now carries $15,355 in credit card debt and $129,579 in total debt.[2] Sean McQuay, NerdWallet's Credit Card Expert, says one reason debt has grown is that the cost of living has outpaced income growth over the past twelve years.

Under Water

Imagine groceries that used to be $184 now $56 more. This increase has happened over the last twelve years. CPI's, or consumer price indexes, measure the price changes of a market basket of consumer goods and services. According to the Bureau of Labor Statistics, the overall CPI went from 184 to 237.945 between 2003 and 2015.

You will decrease your odds of becoming short-sheeted using a faulty short code with a solid financial plan that avoids unreasonable risk.

When the cost of living rises, but your income remains the same, there are necessary adjustments you need to make or your debt level will keep rising. Correspondingly, your stress and relationship tension also rise as financial pressure increases. Do yourself a favor and don't gamble away your savings by taking unsound shortcuts. Look realistically at your finances and how you are managing money. It takes longer to first to seek solid financial advice and put budgeting principles into place, but you will decrease your odds of becoming short-sheeted with a solid financial plan that avoids unreasonable risk. Just as a solid plan works well in your finances, it is well worth the effort in other areas of your personal and professional life.

The Plan! The Plan!

Abraham Lincoln, sixteenth president of the United States (1860-1865), knew the importance of preparation: "Give me six hours to chop down a tree, and I will spend the first four sharpening the ax." The more specific you are in your planning, the more successful you will be. The time spent on planning may feel like wasted effort, but plans are well-worth the investment. The most effective businesses spend a great deal of time planning, but many individuals and small businesses ignore the planning stage and move quickly to the action. Such haste brings undesirable results because of anxiety, ignorance or even unsound advice. Clear communication of a plan makes it easier to make the micro decisions that happen on a daily basis.

Many individuals and small businesses ignore the plan and move quickly to the action with less than desirable results.

It has become easier than ever to put many tasks on autopilot to make your life easier. This is especially true for many of those approaching their middle years. Paul Nussbaum, neuroscientist and cofounder of Fit Brains, the brain-training company bought by Rosetta Stone, says by middle age we run our lives on autopilot. He says most of our day involves "procedural memory." Procedural memory is defined as your "unconcious memory" or your long-term memory. What learning a new language or new musical instrument does is shift you toward new, directed learning.[3] However, it takes committment to a plan.

Stretch Your Brain

More and more studies verify how important it is to stretch your brain in new areas, not just relying on what has become automatic and easy shortcodes. Writing and rewriting books is a skill that definitely stretches my brain. Even though I work at my craft of music composition, production and memorization of new songs to perform, it does not stretch my brain in the same way. Sitting at a piano and playing is second nature to me; in fact in certain situations I carry on complete conversations while continuing to play, even inserting key changes. Cutting down endless paragraphs to make pithy points is not nearly as easy. It takes a great deal of focus, concentration and purposeful action.

In fact, it would be easy to rush, taking a short code because I'm anxious to finish, rushing towards a self imposed deadline. However, the committment to seat discipline during rewrites will make my book manuscripts sharper, clearer and more effective.

It is worthwhile to not take too many short routes as to cut off or misunderstand what could be a complicated message.

Whether in stretching your brain or in financial planning, there are no proven shortcuts to keeping your mind active and working. The same principle applies to any relationship or friendship. Even though you may imagine what the other is thinking or going to say, it is worthwhile to not take too many short routes to cut off or misunderstand what could be a complicated message.

I always enjoy seeing the relationship status on some social media profiles that say "It's complicated." Communicating can be complicated, especially when blending cultures, backgrounds, ethics and styles. Too many short codes in life leave you with a concoction of wires that may never meet and fire without a good plan and method of action.

MINDSETS:

• Avoid disaster with an accurate plan and commitment of time and effort, especially in the areas of finances and personal projects. Don't under-fill the jacuzzi with too many short cuts!

• Mentally affirm you can accomplish more than you imagine. Remember, the human brain inherently performs quicker than a computer and processes more code instantly and seamlessly.

• Commit to stretching your brain in a new area not familiar to you with a plan that includes focus, concentration and purposeful action.

• If you feel as if you have a mental concoction of wires that never meet and fire, stop and develop a good plan and method of action.

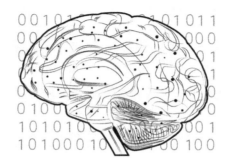

CHAPTER 8

CODE OF CHANGE:
STATIC and DYNAMIC

A small revision in your dynamic mental code alters your ability to modify or transform different areas of your life.

Any small change in computer code will make a huge difference in the ability to see it, revise it or even write it. One basic type of computer code is HTML, used in *static* pages, or pages that stay the same. HTML static code is revised in an editing program, then imported to web pages.

A second type is PHP code, where pages are *dynamic*, or changeable. (Originally called personal home pages) They can be immediately edited, revised and also commented upon without the assistance of an outside editing program. These codes are a good illustration of the static and dynmic codes in life. Since life situations are often dynamic and changing, a small revision in someone's dynamic mental code alters his ability to modify or transform different areas of his life.

Writing New Code

Our son, who during one semester had to write computer code for a college course, compared writing code to writing an essay. However, unlike writing in a Word document, if there are spelling, grammatical or logical errors in the code, the whole essay doesn't work. Also, when writing computer code, instead of writing sentences and paragraphs with letters, he was writing in math equations.

Apparently, reading code is fairly simple compared to writing code. If you have ever read a sentence in a foreign language, compared to actually writing it, you understand why. In reading a sentence, if you understand several keywords that are strung together in a phrase, you can usually decipher and ascertain the basic meaning of the sentence.

However, after crafting a sentence from scratch, you will notice the difference in the way your sentence is put together as compared to a person writing the sentence in her native language. You may feel fairly confident in your ability after your few language classes, but your awkwardly crafted piece of work looks nothing like that of native speakers because the language is not your indigenous language.

If you are not able to craft a plan that works for you, you may not possess the innate ability, or the native language of good code, to do so.

This difference became very apparent to me after writing a song where I inserted a verse in Spanish. My attempt at the language was entirely different than the final version I received from a colleague who spoke the language fluently. In the same way, you may know where you want to be, but you are clumsily stringing the pieces together to reach your goals. If you are not able to craft a plan that works for you, you may not possess the innate ability, or the native language of good code, to do so.

Importance of Syntax

Syntax is the reason it's especially difficult to craft computer code. Syntax is the exact set of rules in the language of code. As an example, in one of my experiments with code, I thought it would be fairly simple to change out just one number in the .php source file. I greatly over-exaggerated my ability. I received an error message when clicking back on my main website and was not able to access my entire website at all until my small error was resolved.

Fortunately, I have on my team a pair of website experts who brought my website back to life almost immediately.[1] Even though I had only changed one numeral in the single .php file, the quotation marks around the revised number required a font change in order for the revision to be correct in the code language.

Incorrect syntax is similar to forgetting the @ in an email address. Or it can be omitting a simple period between a first and last name that makes the address incorrect. Those familiar with email understand how important those details are.

The same principles hold true with reprogramming good code in your life. There are practical elements to create correct virtual code, similar to constructive tools to create good and healthy mental code that will free up your mind to keep moving forward in life.

There are practical elements to create correct virtual code, similar to constructive tools to create good and healthy mental code.

Generating Code

Talent Code is a fairly recent term, coined with the book *Talent Code* by Daniel Coyle.[2] Coyle describes how to bring real talents to light with coaching, motivation and consistent focused practice. Part of the process includes understanding the importance of the myelin sheath in developing new and positive habits.

Myelin wraps around nerve fibers, similarly to rubber wrapping around copper wire, making the nerve signal stronger. With repeated concentrated deep and perfect practice done accurately, the same way each time, each new layer of myelin adds skill and speed, reinforcing the desired skill faster.[3]

I didn't realize it until later in my career, but using the principles of perfect practice and the myelin sheath was how I was trained as a concert pianist. My instructor was very specific and strict on hand position and relaxation, insisting on repetitive practice done the correct way with multiple rhythms and different memorization techniques.

Understanding the science of the myelin sheath is a very important tool that can be used for developing new habits with repetition. It's also an extremely beneficial tool in the process of changing bad mental code into good mental code. (This concept will be discussed more in-depth later in this book.)

Bad Mental Code

To recognize bad mental code, it is helpful to first recognize good mental code. The same principle holds true when dealing with currency and money. To recognize real and counterfeit bills, workers are trained with real currency; everything from coins to all types of large bills.

To recognize bad mental code, it is helpful to first recognize good mental code.

In America, Colonial paper currency designed and printed on the 1756 note by Benjamin Franklin and others bore the phrase "to counterfeit is death."[4] Nations have used counterfeiting as a means of warfare so the real value of the dollar plummets. For instance, the U.S. dollar is the standard for much of the current world's currency. If it is artificially devalued or replaced in any way, entire grids of commerce could unravel and crash.

Bad code takes on many different forms. In this book, bad mental code will be referred to as the code that will counterfeit or hinder you from moving forward in your personal and professional life, unraveling the grid of your life. It can act as the negative self-talk that poisons a positive and hopeful attitude. It can take on the form of bitterness, anger and resentment, all of which grow into ominous roadblocks in life that are difficult to overcome unless they are confronted and changed. Bad code can also take on the emotion of paralyzing fear, inhibiting you from making any change to move forward.

Good Mental Code

To identify good mental code is not quite so simple. Some of the traits of bad code can actually be used as warning signs and keep you from toxic relationships and situations. However, the negative code still needs confronted and modified.

Studying every part of good healthy mental code will help in turning even what appears like a negative trait into a positive. With computer-generated code, distinguishing good and bad code is never straightforward. Because of that reality, the demand for cyber-security professionals is exploding in the virtual realm of code. The demand for trained individuals outweighs the current supply.

Cyber-terrorism is hard to stop because there's no real consistent test to know what is malicious and harmful, that can spread a virus on every web page. However, there are signals to recognize what isn't normal and at times, trails to distinguish where a particular code originated.

In the same way, identifying the source of the code, whether good or bad, will be useful in making any changes. Good mental code in your life gives you the ability to develop confidence, peace, and a sense of purpose. It also encourages positive self-talk, which is instrumental in dealing with the many changes the years bring throughout the decades of your life.

Positive Steps

The good news is, just as looking at a glass half full will give you hope, understanding positive steps and methods to rid your life of destructive bad mental code is truly possible. You can change "I cant" to "I can." Just as vulnerabilities exist on every type of cyber information system, our lives contain vulnerable areas if protections are not in place. Living life is dynamic as it changes constantly, but you may have static areas and attitudes that will hinder your personal growth without a willingness to change.

Just as vulnerabilities exist on every type of cyber information system, our lives contain vulnerable areas if protections are not in place.

You must be willing to not only evaluate your personal dynamic and static code, but to make positive code corrections for anything in this book to really help you. After doing so, I know you will find some areas and principles that will propel you forward in your journey of personal and professional growth.

 MINDSETS:

• Identify a small revision in your dynamic mental code that will alter your ability to modify or transform an area of your life. This can be as simple as repeating "I can" instead of "I can't."

• Recognize and identify the main traits of good mental code in your life.

• Analyze every part of the good healthy mental code you possess to turn even what seems like a negative into a positive.

• Identify static areas and attitudes that will hinder your personal growth. You must have a willingness to change and a firm resolve to change those attitudes.

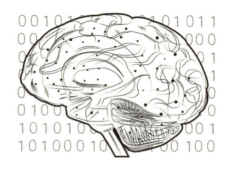

CHAPTER 9

CODE OF ENTRY: ENCRYPTION

The brain acts like an encryption device, deciphering sounds, smells and visual images, hindering certain types of good or bad code.

To date, gas crews have installed 2,606 air purification systems and 820 plug-in systems. They've also weatherized 2,245 homes in Porter Ranch, California, all because of a natural gas leak. The leak, which is estimated by the Environmental Defense Fund to have spewed close to 100,000 tons of greenhouse gas methane in the atmosphere, has sickened many residents, displaced more than 4,000 households and prompted the relocation of students at two schools.[1] The source of the leak was a metal pipe in a breached seven inch casing. The safety valve was removed and not replaced.

Is there an indication of a gas leak in your life? Maybe you can pinpoint a time where you let your guard down with someone in a work or personal relationship, by speaking or lashing out with anger or fear you later regretted. You may have made some unwise financial decisions on a whim in your past, not listening to the wise words of an advisor, so that later on you are still paying for the mistake and feel trapped by your errors.

How about your physical health? Rationalization, temptation, and excuses are all open doors of mental vulnerability, similar to a gas leak with no safety valve. Encryption prevents unwanted visitors on virtual sites and is a good example of smart protection. In the same way, you put protections in place for your home, personal belongings and personal passwords.

Compromised Security

The first step in creating positive and lasting change with good mental code comes with an honest look at the source of the problem. After identifying the cause or the basis of the leak, you can take necessary steps to replace the bad code with good code.

The first step in creating positive and lasting change with good mental code comes with an honest look at the source of the problem.

There must be an entry point with any threat of compromised security. If someone wanted to break into your home, they could do so, even through your front door. You may have alarms, cameras and extra lighting that will hinder an intruder. However, with an axe, a sledgehammer or some type of weapon or car, a person could break down your door and enter. Even with deterrents, no entry is totally safe. The same holds true with a cyber attack and bad malicious code.

The Porter Ranch gas leak occurred because a safety valve was removed and not replaced. This would be similar to taking the old locks off your doors, but never replacing them with newer locks, more secure and stable. Most would not consider neglecting locks in their home or office. However, ignorance and disregard for your positive mental code and habits can be just as dangerous.

Cyber Attacks

A cyber attack is the attempt by hackers to damage or destroy a computer network or system. There is a real possibility that you or someone close to you will face a cyber attack sometime in your lifetime. Even if you are a small business or entrepreneur, a cyber attack can cost you customers or sales and thwart your efforts in any number of ways. The Sony Pictures cyber attack in 2015 was first reported to cost the company $15 million, but the figure went up to $35 million for IT repairs.[2]

Sony is large enough that it expects no significant harm from the cyber attack in the long run, but that is not the case for everyone facing an attack. Even the health insurance giant, *Anthem,* was hit with a massive cyber attack in 2015 that put close to eighty million customers at risk of identity theft: "Hacks like this are unfortunately commonplace," Robert Siciliano, an online safety expert to Intel Security, told ABC News.

A cyber attack is similar to the bad code of corrupted thinking, infecting everything else in your life unless you meet it head-on.

The information highway is growing at warp speed and dependence on connection and technology is at the cusp of exploding. It has become absolutely necessary to understand protections you need to put in place, not only for your business, but your personal life. A cyber attack is similar to the bad code of corrupted thinking, infecting everything else in your life unless you meet it head-on. For example, telling yourself you're too old or not smart enough to learn a new skill. That's just not true!

Protecting Your Assets

Many have some sort of deterrent online, whether a firewall on a computer or password access. Firewalls are like filters that reject traffic based on specific rules. They are especially prevalent in the financial services and medical fields. In regards to sharing personal information, it's daunting at times to know exactly what to share and how safe a site is. Most secure websites that begin with *https* are still relatively safe for sharing information.

However, even privacy acts and symbols of secure transactions may send a false sense of security. Then, at an unexpected time, you are hit, "BAM!" with an unexpected attack or identity theft.

False Security

Who would guess an organization as large as *Target* would not have proper protections in place? In mid-December 2013, criminals forced their way into Target's system, gaining access to guest credit and debit card information. The information included names, mailing addresses, email addresses or phone numbers. They found that up to seventy million individuals were affected.[3]

It was discovered that the breach occurred when hackers stole private information from a trusted third party vendor, a refrigeration, heating and air conditioner subcontractor.[4] Apparently, the real problem occurred because Target was so certain their customer information was safe that they didn't bother encrypting secure information. All that private customer information was just waiting for the hackers to feast upon, just like the plethora of food at a cruise buffet is available for traveler's consumption.

Many live with a false sense of security, not only in cyberspace, but in their personal and professional lives. All it takes is not having safeguards in place one time. It is a harsh wake-up call to be blasted with the demons of discouragement, devastation of theft and violation of privacy. Just like a slow underground leak that spreads toxic gas, attacks can leave you crippled with the bad mental code of incapacitating fear or arouse you to sprint with the positive action of creating the good mental code of realistic goals.

Securing Your Assets

Encryption is the conversion of information from a readable state to apparent nonsense. This prevents unwanted persons from accessing information meant for a specific recipient. If a company or organization has not encrypted secure information, your credit or personal information may be obtained with a purchase or other transaction. Encryption is one of the best safeguards an individual can use to help prevent their data from falling into the wrong hands.[5]

Encryption is in place every time you have to use a secret key or password to access a network. It is in place when you have to sign on to use your computer or even unlock your phone. Encryption is like an iron-gate around your front door, making it more difficult for hackers to enter. In the same way, securing the right tools to keep bad mental code out of your life acts as an extra barrier and encrypted safeguard.

Brain Power

The brain acts like an encryption device, deciphering sounds, smells and visual images, hindering certain types of good or bad code. The brain translates thousands of different types of code every day into understandable sights and messages. It's hard to imagine an encryption machine more sophisticated than the human brain. Three pounds of brain tissue hold about eighty-six billion neurons, cells that fire split-second electrical pulses to stimuli.[6]

The real-life story of Alan Turing inspired the award-winning movie *The Imitation Game*, the highest grossing independent film of 2014. The movie was all about breaking the German Enigma code the Nazis used to provide security for their radio messages. Turing's contributions and mental genius significantly shortened the war and saved thousands of lives.[7]

Guard your mind with constructive thoughts, looking at areas that could be entry points for defeat, putting encryption tools in place.

Most don't understand the huge capacity of the brain and its power. Understanding the brain and the myelin sheath make it possible to create positive and lasting change with the constructive repetition of good code. Guard your mind with constructive thoughts, honestly looking at areas that could be entry points for defeat, putting encryption tools in place. Some of those areas can include better self control, anger management, people skills, consistency in weight and health issues.

MINDSETS:

• Evaluate and identify an area of your life where you may face a mental slow gas leak that will develop into bad mental code. This may include a negative, corrupted way of thinking, infecting relationships and attitudes about your career.

• Don't live with a false sense of security, either in cyberspace or in your personal and professional lives. Secure your virtual assets as well as guard your mental thoughts.

• Guard your mind with constructive thoughts, honestly looking at areas that could be entry points for defeat, putting encryption tools in place. Remember, the brain acts like an encryption device, deciphering sounds, smells and visual images, hindering certain types of good or bad code.

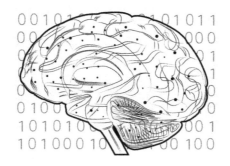

CHAPTER 10

CODE OF ATTACK: PHISHING

What looks perfectly fine and legitimate on the outside can be dangerous and destructive on the inside.

Today, it's not if, but when you'll face a cyber attack. That statement alone confirms the importance of being prepared. Just as a cyber attack inserts a virus or bad code into a computer or network, the brain has an entry point, letting in the bad code of discouragement, anger and failure into your mental thoughts.

When you understand the types of cyber attacks and bad code, you can plan your strategy to combat and resist those attacks. In the game *Battleship*, (Hasbro toys) players try to guess the location of their opponent's ships located on a grid. Studying the areas where an attack can happen will help one win the game. The same principle holds true of a phishing cyber attack or attack of bad mental code.

Recognize the Origin

My website was working just fine until I started running out of memory capacity, or CPU. It was extremely puzzling and I read many articles that suggested it could be the plug-ins on my website. I tested and tested, eliminating one plug-in after another and searched out a number of online forums and informational feeds with no definite solution. One thing I knew for certain was that I had not been hacked again, so that was a relief. My website was clean.

What I finally discovered was that my particular website theme, which I loved, contained many bells and whistles, with multiple sliders that were very attractive. Sliders allow users to insert a number of photos that will automatically fade in and out. However, these features also use up memory space.

I'm a creative soul and when I started evaluating my website, I found that I had used those memory-gobbling sliders on over a dozen pages. I had no way of really knowing if the storage problem would be solved until I disabled the sliders.

Visual Snapshots

To disable the sliders took some work. I took a snapshot of every web page, as I knew I'd need to reformat every page where a former slider had been. All my work paid off after literally doing surgery on my website. I was able to disable and remove the slider plug-ins from my main plug-ins and reformat my web pages.

My point in all this is that it may take some time to first define the problem. I knew about the types of cyber and other attacks, but I had to find what was affecting my particular website. In the same way, you may know about bad mental code, but need to discover how it's affecting you in some particular or unique way.

You may know about bad mental code, but need to discover how it's affecting you in some particular or unique way.

Unfortunately, disabling the sliders didn't totally solve my problem, but it was a step in the right direction. To take a step in the right direction in your life may involve digging deep to find vulnerable personal and professional regions. Taking mental or visual snapshots of varying aspects of your life is a helpful tool to reveal areas of required change.

Personal Miscalculations

Two small Rivertine Navy boats drifted into Iran territorial waters on Monday, January 11, 2016. There was speculation as to why this happened, from mechanical problems in their navigation system, to actual mechanical failure. After the ten sailors were returned safely, they admitted that part of the problem was a navigational error. There may have been mechanical failure on top of that, but the incident happened because of miscalculation.[1]

You can blame many problems on attacks and misguided information, but be brave and courageous enough to understand and admit your own margin of error or personal miscalculation. Also be willing to look for any weak links, whether in your personal or professional relationships, your systems, your time management or other areas including health or finances. Just as taking snapshots on a computer can help you look at a situation under a different light, taking mental snapshots of different aspects of your life will help you identify areas of possible miscalculation. For example, it feels good to create new innovative products, but an honest evaluation of what is selling will help you stay afloat. This is especially relevant in area of the arts, as funds can easily swirl down an endless sinkhole without realistic assessment of products and projects.

Be brave and courageous enough to understand and admit your own margin of error or personal miscalculation.

Phishing

Recently, I received a message from *PayPal* stating there was a client payment of $50 that needed verification. Even though the email looked completely legitimate, I wasn't certain I had anything I was selling for exactly that amount. Although it was very tempting to access the easy-to-click link in the email, I signed into my PayPal account directly from my browser. There I found no questionable charge, so I knew the email probably contained a form of malware.

What looks perfectly fine and legitimate on the outside can be dangerous and destructive on the inside. When a fraudulent email attempts to obtain personal information, such as usernames, password details and credit card details, it's called phishing. These websites masquerade as legitimate sources. The logos look real and they seem to contain all the right information.

Some self-help programs act like phishing and look totally valid.

In the same way, some easy-to-access self-help programs are tempting to access and follow. There are easy steps to get rich, stress-free guides to weight loss, seven to ten simple steps to build a successful business and plenty more promises of success. Some self-help programs act like phishing and look totally valid. However, many don't give completely legitimate information, luring you and hooking you into a program that may or may not be appropriate in order to gather your personal information and take your money!

Even though many of those programs are not spreading malware, they can lure you away from finding a true solution in replacing bad and unhealthy code, thus wasting your valuable time, effort and even resources. An even more targeted approach than phishing is a spear phishing attack.

Spear Phishing vs. Spearfishing

Whereas ordinary phishing involves malicious emails sent to any random email account, spear phishing emails are designed to appear to come from someone the recipient knows and trusts—such as a colleague, business manager or human resource department—and includes a subject line or content that is specifically tailored to the victim's known interests or industry. These are extremely popular and thus, even more dangerous to open.

The term spearfishing is an ancient method of fishing in a body of water. Spearfishing started with spearing fish from rivers and streams using sharpened sticks. Today, modern spearfishing makes use of elastic powered spearguns and slings, or compressed gas pneumatic powered spearguns to strike the hunted fish.

George "Doc" Lopez, founder and former CEO of the Board of ICU Medical, Inc., currently holds the world record for the largest black marlin ever caught spearfishing without scuba gear, which is 269.4 lbs.[2] To spear a fish that large, the aim of the speargun needs to be exact and targeted. The same principle holds true for spear phishing in the virtual world. The target is exact and many times, the catch is rather large.

Grandma's Retirement

Spear Phishing has the potential to take all your grandmother's retirement. I distinctly remember when my mother-in-law received an email asking for a great deal of money because her grandson (my nephew) was in trouble. She was extremely worried and concerned, mainly because the email was so specific in detail, so she was afraid to tell anyone. The instructions were for her to keep absolutely silent about the situation. Fortunately she mentioned it to a neighbor who alerted the family.

My father was also the recent victim of a scam. He was told his grandson (another nephew!) was in jail and could be released with $2,000, all in the form of gift cards. Of course, everything had to be hush-hush. When my dad was relaying this story to me, when he got to the part about finding the closest Toys 'R Us to purchase the gift cards, before I could say "No! You didn't!" he said he had written the check.

Through a few prayers, providence and divine intervention, he was not out an additional $25,000, although he was extremely close. I say all this not to be critical, but there are those in your life who love you so much that they will do anything for you. Some of those people are a generation or two ahead of you so they don't understand these types of scams and should be educated about the dangers. Truly, it could be your grandmother's, or grandfather's retirement at stake.

For really valued and affluent victims, attackers may even study *Facebook*, *LinkedIn* and other social networking sites to gain intelligence and personal information about a victim. They then choose the names of trusted people in their target's network to impersonate, or bring up a topic of interest to gain trust. By doing so, they seek to gain unauthorized access to confidential data.[3] The scammer knew my father's address and even put a person on the phone who sounded like my nephew.

Just as there are scams of spear-phishing attacks in the virtual world, there are targeted attacks on your mind, as it is the most powerful computer in the universe.

Many of the spear-phishing emails also contain an attachment that will spread a virus or malware when opened. All this is mentioned not to increase panic, but to encourage you to be on guard. Every generation, back to ancient times, has experienced some sort of scam. It's just the type of scam that has changed with a different format and style.

Just as there are scams of spear-phishing attacks in the virtual world, there are targeted attacks on your mind, as it is the most powerful computer in the universe. If not careful, your brain will be caught off guard in areas of vulnerability in unexpected ways and times. So be on guard!

 MINDSETS:

• Take mental or visual snapshots of different aspects of your life as a helpful tool that will reveal areas of required change.

• Be aware that what looks perfectly fine and legitimate on the outside can be dangerous and destructive on the inside.

• Stay away from programs that lure you away from finding a true solution in replacing bad and unhealthy code, thus wasting your valuable time, effort and even resources. These can include programs that claim you will get rich quick, lose weight with little or no effort, or boost your metabolism with a simple healthy drink or pill.

• Be vigilant. In the same way as there are scams of spear-phishing attacks in the virtual world, there are targeted attacks on your mind, as it is the most powerful computer in the universe.

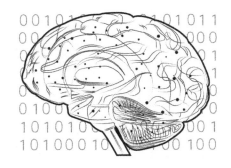

CHAPTER 11

CODE OF DESTRUCTION: MALWARE

Malware is just like letting the worm of bad mental code in your life, creating chaos and destruction.

The five-pound box of chocolates had been sitting on top of the upright piano in our living room for months. Every time my sister and I walked by the box, we eyed it, wondering why it hadn't been eaten.

One day when our mother left on an errand, we decided to dig into that box, eating just a few pieces each. What could it hurt? As we did, we got a bit carried away and enjoyed quite a few pieces on several layers, then put the box back, rearranging the papers and chocolates inside to try to minimize the damage of our splurging. Possibly some of you have done something similar, perhaps not with chocolates, but with some other tempting item. Little did we know what disruption eating those chocolates would have on our psyche, acting just like malware.

Chaos and Destruction

A day later, our mother approached us, questioning who had gotten into the candy box. Even though there were no remnants of chocolate smeared over our faces, we knew we couldn't totally cover up what we had done. We admitted to eating the delicious morsels, with the justification that we couldn't understand why the box was left unattended so long, uneaten. With a small grin, she said, "Because I was going to return them. The candies had worms." Suddenly, we both felt sick, as what looked delicious on the outside wasn't what was hidden inside.

Malware operates the same way. On the outside, an attachment can look perfectly legitimate. However, upon opening, you may find a worm that can wreak havoc. Malware is just like letting the worm of bad mental code in your life, creating chaos and destruction.

Malware and Worms

Malware is malicious software that may look perfectly safe on the outside, but contains sophisticated attachments that burrow deep into computer network operating systems. All it takes is for one computer in a network to access a wrong website or click on a link that contains malware and the whole network could be unprotected, vulnerable to outside access.

Any type of malware brings danger for secure files and company secrets. The theft of intellectual property has become rampant and much of that property has been accessed with malicious software. Malware creators change the outward appearance of their attacking programs using camouflage techniques.[1] What may look like a legitimate link and email may be disguised with the colors, the logos and the language of the legitimate website. It would be similar to the *PayPal* email I received that looked official but was really a counterfeit site meant to steal my login information. Such fake messages can also infect computers with viruses or a worm. You might feel fairly safe, but with a sophisticated phishing or spear phishing attack, you might be as vulnerable as the city of Troy.

Story of Troy

The story of Troy goes back to the Trojan War in the 13th or 12th century B.C. with the Greeks constructing a huge wooden horse, and hiding a select force of men inside. As the Greeks pretended to sail away, the Trojans pulled the horse into their city as a victory trophy. You know the rest of the story. That night, the Greek forces crept out of the horse and opened the gates for the rest of the Greek army, which had sailed back to fight and win the war.

You might feel fairly safe, but with a sophisticated phishing or spear phishing attack, you might be as vulnerable as the city of Troy.

In today's language, a Trojan horse is a malicious computer program, appearing useful, routine or interesting in order to persuade a victim to install it. The Trojan horse in computer terms does the same damage as the disguised Trojan wooden horse. The hidden computer program is brought on your computer and opened up to release an entire army of bad code. What was masked as legitimate proved to be extremely damaging.

Certain thoughts and actions in your personal and professional life can also be disguised as legitimate. Holding a grudge may seem perfectly valid until it damages personal or business relationships with hate that eats you up inside. Procrastination about weight or health may be justifiable and reasonable until you face an unexpected heart attack, onset of diabetes or other health issue. Each of those could be a game-changer in your life, with you being caught off guard just as the Trojan horse surprised its victims.

Certain thoughts and actions in your personal and professional life may be disguised as legitimate, just as a Trojan horse.

Rummaging Through your Closets

Surprise attacks are not the only real and present danger; hacking is also dangerous in the cyber and personal world. If you have ever had your credit card information taken and exploited, faced identity theft or dealt with a virus on your computer, you understand the hassle and extra time it takes to resolve those issues. In addition, as an invasion of privacy, it feels as if someone broke in your home and rummaged through your personal underwear and closets.

An estimated ninety-one percent of hacking attacks begin with phishing or spear-phishing emails.

We are vulnerable on many fronts. The first electronic mail was sent in 1971. Now, almost forty trillion emails are sent a year. With trillions of possibilities, hackers look at the ocean of phishing possibilities and start casting. An estimated ninety-one percent of hacking attacks begin with phishing or spear-phishing emails.[2]

Fighting the Battle

Ninety-seven percent of Fortune 500 companies have been hacked and more than one hundred governments are gearing up to fight battles in the online domain.[3] In fact, the National Cyber Security Division has doubled or tripled in size every year since its inception.[4] Just as hacking is prevalent in the virtual world of computers, hacking will happen in your life and business if you don't have proper mental safeguards in place. You will be in danger of a surprise attack. Remember, the human brain is a massive encryption device and just as computers can be hacked with bad code, so can your mind.

The human brain is a massive encryption device and just as computers can be hacked with bad code, so can your mind.

61

In the fictional novel *Ghost Ship* by Clive Cussler,[5] when characters became aware their main computers were hacked and manipulated, the rescue operation went completely off line. Once the hackers had accessed the complete communication system to follow their victims' every move, the new orders to the commanders came through old-fashioned typewriters and hand-carried notes. Even in a novel like Cussler's, the words of Oscar Wilde ring true, "Life imitates art far more than art imitates life." It was a drastic move in the fictional story to turn off computers, but it demonstrates viable extreme measures in taking a step back to depend on a trusted source to solve a problem.

Though it's tempting to take shortcuts, you may need to take a similar drastic course in your life. For our individual use in preventing bad code, it is best to develop a double layer of protection. How do you do that? With computers it's by cryptography or cryptology, which is the practice and study of techniques for secure information.

Cryptography or Cryptology

Modern cryptography is based on mathematical theory and computer science practice. This makes the algorithms, or sets of rules for problem solving, hard to break by any adversary. You don't need to understand the math but just that public key encryption is the very best form of protection and is mostly used by big business in exchanging data. There are two levels of passwords in public key encryption. The first is a public password, with access to everyone. The second is private and changes with each transaction.

If you give your house key out to everyone you meet, that is the first public key encryption. However, if there is another key that changes constantly to gain access behind a first door: that is the private access that provides another layer of protection. This would be similar to placing a locked gate in front of your front door, or bars in front of windows, with two separate keys for each entrance. There are now two layers of security.

Home security cameras have become increasingly popular, gaining even more recognition with remote access, many times with multiple "eyes" that view property from a number of angles. A camera alone is not recommended as a sole component of defense. However, it will help identify any movement at any entrances, which establishes valuable information in knowing who and what to respond to.

When I started writing my first book, *Stuck is Not a Four Letter Word*,[6] I found one of the most difficult tasks was to find legitimate trusted sources for information I discovered online, or even in books and magazines. I found quotes and facts, but many that had no citations to the original research or information. There were bits of information disguised as legitimate, yet upon further exploration, there was no solid research to confirm the facts. Some of the quotes were convincing in flashy one-sheets and blogs. However, it reminded me of a salesperson at my front door who was repeatedly knocking to enter my house. I had protections in place to allow me to see if the source of the knock was legitimate and trusted. I took the same action with my book, spending several days to document and confirm valid quoted information.

A valid source of information as well as a solid double encryption of protection serve to protect your mental thoughts to prevent bad code.

Recognizing valid sources of information in composing a book is similar to recognizing who or what is about to enter your property with a good security camera. If you then add a double layer of protection with locks, you are still able to see what or who is trying to enter, choosing whether or not it is a legitimate source or guest. The same principle holds true with your mental code. A valid trusted source of information as well as a solid double encryption of protection serve to protect your mental thoughts to prevent the worms or army of bad mental code.

MINDSETS:

• Be vigiliant with your thoughts as they lead to action. Once you let the worm of bad mental code in your life, such as unresolved bitterness, anger or jealousy, you have opened the door to chaos and destruction.

• Identify thoughts and actions in your personal and professional life that can be disguised as legitimate, but are spurious.

• Put mental safeguards in place. Safeguards include checking valid sources of information, attitudes and risks associated with projects. Just as hacking is prevalent in the virtual world of computers, hacking will happen in your life and business if you don't have proper mental safeguards in place.

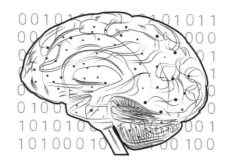

CHAPTER 12

CODE OF PERSISTENCE: BRUTE FORCE

*Understand there will be change, so put protections in place
to be able to meet and accept that change,
both virtually and mentally.*

Brute force attacks are very persistent, similar to the actions of one of our dogs who was a portrait of determination. We had two small poodles named Sparky and Spunky. (Our sons didn't call them *real* dogs!) Spunky was older, smaller and all black, except for a white patch on his stomach. He also had a long tongue, which hung out of the right side of his mouth most of the time, not giving him a look of intelligence.

Spunky was the most tenacious dog I've ever encountered. If he wanted in or out of a room, he would scratch on the door until someone responded. His scraping at the door would last for hours if not acknowledged. It was totally annoying. There were days we just left the door open because we didn't want to be bothered. His tenaciousness was similar to a brute force attack.

Similarly, some people leave the door open with data and personal information, as well as mental thoughts. It's inconvenient and sometimes annoying and difficult to always be on the alert, closing the door. However, an open door, whether in a home, mental thoughts or on a computer increase the likelihood of an attack.

On Your Guard

If public key encryption is so strong in the computer world, why are there still so many vulnerabilities, identity thefts, and data breaches? This warning is not meant to scare or panic anyone, but it is a fact of life in our society. If you lived at the turn of the century (1900), were frozen, and awakened 100 years later, seeing a modern car, a plane or train would be shocking and maybe even cause one to wish to return back to a frozen state as the changes would be mind-boggling!

Present-age technology is moving much quicker than the early 1900's, but the principles are the same. Understand there will be change, so put protections in place to be able to meet and accept that change, both virtually and mentally. Part of being ready for change is the ability to understand several areas of vulnerability. We will look at a couple of those areas of attack, which also have applicable principles to apply to your mental code.

Brute Force

A brute force attack is an exhaustive search where the attacker systematically checks all possible keys or passwords until the correct one is found. Brute force might be used when it is not possible to take advantage of other weaknesses in an encryption system. As the password's length increases, the amount of time, on average, to find the correct password increases exponentially. This means short passwords can usually be discovered quite quickly, but longer passwords may take decades.

It takes work to prevent a brute force attack, by making sure passwords are up-to-date and protected. Some days, it's just more convenient to leave the door open, just as we did at times for Spunky. The same vigilance holds true with your mental thoughts. Some days it's easier to let your guard down and eat everything in sight, not realizing the box of chocolates may have worms. Or you may give up when the work force and technology changes start to leave you behind, justifying you're too old or too tired to learn a new skill.

Neglect Doesn't Pay

In 2005, Joe Lopez, a Florida businessman, filed a suit against Bank of America after hackers stole $90,000 from his Bank of America account. The money had been transferred to Latvia, a country in Northern Europe. An investigation showed that Mr. Lopez's computer was infected with malware, which recorded every keystroke and sent the information to malicious users via the internet. The hackers got hold of Joe Lopez's user name and password so the court did not rule in favor of Mr. Lopez. Why? The court said that Mr. Lopez had neglected to take basic precautions when managing his bank account, and he had not updated his antivirus protection for over two years.[1]

Key logging or keyboard capturing is the action of recording (logging) the keys struck on a keyboard covertly, so that the person using the keyboard is unaware that their actions are being monitored. Key logging malware can reside in an operating system, undetected by the user. The danger lies in opening any email or attachment from an unverified or unknown source.

The annoying messages you receive of automatic security or antivirus updates on your computer are there for a reason—to protect your property against new attacks. In fact, my managed WordPress website just sent me a message they had removed a plug-in because of issues with performance and security.

The minor obstacles you are facing today may hold
significant consequences down the road.

Just as virtual updates can be a nuisance, the updates on your personal information about your health, fitness and other areas of life are just as important. Those types of messages, such as borderline diabetes, stroke risks and looming bankruptcy are usually sent for a good reason. In a fast paced society, it's easy to ignore them, but the minor obstacles you are facing today may hold significant consequences down the road.

Stealth Attacks

A recent article stated that while Brian Wallace was on the trail of hackers who had snatched a California university's housing files, he stumbled into a larger nightmare. Cyber attackers had opened a pathway into the networks running the United States power grid.[2]

Digital clues pointed to Iranian hackers and Wallace found that they had already taken passwords, as well as engineered drawings of dozens of power plants. The drawings were so detailed that experts say skilled attackers could have used them, along with other tools and malicious code, to knock out electricity to millions of homes.

You want to be stealth because when you need to do
something you are already in place.

Many reports like Wallace's are never reported publically, but the threat of these types of intrusions definitely exists. "You want to be stealth," said Lillian Ablon, a cybersecurity expert at the RAND Corp. "That's the ultimate power, because when you need to do something you are already in place."

B-2 Bomber

Many of the current power systems across the U.S. are old and were not built with network security in mind. Likewise, many of you have also not set up systems in your business or in personal lives that can withstand stealth attacks. A stealth attack is one that is undetected on a computer. They are "undercover." The term "stealth attack" is taken from the B-2 bomber, also known as the stealth bomber. It is a 172-foot wide revolutionary machine, nearly invisible to enemy sensors. These amazing aircraft often fly over major events such as the Rose Parade or Super Bowl.

As I discuss areas of vulnerability in this book, realize that in our world, future wars will not just be fought by soldiers with guns or with planes dropping bombs. They will also be fought with the click of a mouse half a world away, unleashing carefully weaponized computer programs.[3] Remember that behind all computer and virtual technology exists the greatest physical computer of all, the human brain which is not invincible, but powerful. It will help you in fighting wars of your mind as you expose areas of weakness.

Areas of Vulnerability

In replacing bad code with good code, whether on a computer or in the mind, it is important to first identify areas of vulnerability. My own website was hacked because I did not have solid protection in place on my comment forms. This allowed a bot (robotic search engine spider) to enter and place a virus in the .php file of one of my main pages, and the damage spread from there like wild fire.

This has a great personal application. You will often be caught off guard if you don't realize areas of weakness using periscopic eyes. How often have you failed at dieting, finishing a work project, meeting your monthly business budget or in some aspect of your personal life? Can you pinpoint why? Maybe there are small areas, or contact points, that are open to thoughts of justification, apathy, discouragement, fear, or other dangerous types of viruses and bad code that can spread riotously, leaving you paralyzed or ineffective.

After understanding how bad code attacks, you can apply further safeguards of protection that will work for you. Remember, your brain deciphers encryption faster than a computer, but it needs to be focused and protected from malware and viruses that fly in like a stealth bomber.

After understanding how bad code happens, you can apply further safeguards of protection that will work for you.

 MINDSETS:

• Define areas of your life where you are vulnerable. Some may include finances, self confidence, apathy or fear.

• Identify a pattern of vigilance for your mental thoughts. Be open to new ideas and thoughts, but be on guard for shortcuts and attacks that will discourage and destroy your enthusiasm and progress. Negativity can creep in like a brute force attack, so don't leave your mental door open.

• Don't be afraid of using future technology, just prepare yourself with the tools available to you. In our world, future wars will not just be fought by soldiers with guns or with planes that drop bombs. They will also be fought with the click of a mouse half a world away that unleashes carefully weaponized computer programs.

• Remember, your brain is the most powerful computer of all and is open to attacks that fly in like a stealth bomber. You will often be caught off guard if you don't realize areas of weakness using periscopic eyes.

PART TWO
TOOLS OF CODE

How to Repair
Bad Code

CHAPTER 13

POWERFUL TOOL:
PATCH and SNAKED CHUTE

*Safeguarding yourself against malware of the mind with security
updates, patches and mental power saws
are powerful mental tools.*

In addressing how to repair bad code, this section employs construction images to help you picture how to apply various mental tools. In a construction job, if you need to remove a slab of cement, you can either use a sledgehammer or a jackhammer. You are in control of both tools but one exerts a great deal more power and pressure than the other.

The two main powerful tools mentioned here provide the basic foundation of your toolbox. The first is a powerful patch, for drywall, brick or other type of material. The importance of a patch in repairing computer systems cannot be underestimated, as it is a file that is directly inserted to replace corrupted code. It illustrates the power in replacing the vulnerabilities that lead to bad mental code. The second is a power saw, illustrating what it takes to carve a new path with a willingness to change, illustrated by a curved, or snaked chute used by cattle. Those two powerful tools will start you off in assembling your personal toolbox.

Areas of Vulnerability

A single vulnerability, just like an unlocked door is not really a threat if no one wants to enter. However, one unprotected area will lead to many regions and open entrances if not addressed. Our bodies and minds have hundreds of subcomponents that interact, just as modern computer operating systems have millions of lines of code and entry points.

If you understand the underlying goals and habits of attackers, you will be better prepared to protect and eliminate threats. Athletes study their opponents in detail for any area of weakness. Even though every game brings surprises and unexpected plays, they are well prepared to react with more precision and confidence in playing the game with thorough preparation.

A computer hacker's goal is to find some chink in the armor of the code. Computers, just like your mind, use memory to store data and instructions. If a computer program can be tricked into writing data that is different than needed, your mind can also be tricked with faulty commands. The remedy is a patch, a piece of computer software designed to update or fix a computer program, including security vulnerabilities and bugs. It is an executable file, which means it is inserted directly into the program to replace the damaged code. The increased demand for patch management reflects the expansion and dependence on virtual communication in life and business, which can come to a standstill if controlled by faulty code.

Held Ransom

A classic example of vulnerability occured when the Hollywood Presbyterian Medical Center went ten days before noticing malware in its computer system: it's ability to access any patient records was ultimately disabled. The ransom price was forty bitcoins, or about $17,000 to the hackers who infiltrated and immobilized its computer network. Hospital CEO Allen Stefanek said in a statement, "Paying the ransom was the quickest and most efficient way to restore most of our systems and administrative functions." The hospital said patient care wasn't compromised, though the cyber attack forced the facility to temporarily revert to paper registrations and medical records.[1]

Tracing ransom attacks is extremely difficult. There's not much local law enforcement can do, especially when overseas criminals commit these types of crimes. Also, bitcoin can't be traced, different than many other types of currency.

How this attack occured is through CryptoLocker, known as "ransomware." It is a relatively common type of malware that reaches to outside servers, usually coming from overseas sources: it downloads encryption instructions, (bad codes) that scramble a computer's contents, making them inaccessible to anyone without a specific "key." It can move through an entire computer network, keeping users from accessing any of their files.

Your mental data or thoughts can also be held ransom and keep you from never accessing your full potential. Mental ransomware may come from your family background which contained messages that you are not good or smart enough to pursue your dreams. In school or at work, you may have an internal imbedded memo that you will never be able to learn certain subjects or do a particular task well. Those feelings need to be replaced with a mental patch that will override the missives that are holding you back. For example, replace shame with self-respect of who you are as a person. Insert an approach of lifelong learning with defined goals for your future in place of an attitude of failure. For business, inserting a patch of a constructive mindset or attitude will turn a standstill into positive movement.

Your mental data or thoughts can be held ransom
to never access your full potential.

When a drywall patch is replaced and smoothed, there is usually no visible seam. To replace a mental patch is not as easy as some drywall patches, but it can function just as smoothly when inserted and functioning correctly. It will give you a new level of assurance and confidence against the ransomware of mental vulnerability as you face your past as well as your future.

Who's Driving Your Car?

Chrysler Auto had a well publicized wake-up call with hacking issues on their vehicles, which prompted a sweeping recall of over 1.4 million vehicles. Two technology researchers had hacked wirelessly into a Jeep Cherokee through its dashboard connectivity system. They managed to gain control of not just features like the radio and air-conditioning, but the actual functions of the car: the engine, the brakes and the steering.[2]

Fiat Chrysler software specialists scrambled to make a patch available to plug the hole of vulnerability after Andy Greenberg was driving 70 mph on the edge of downtown St. Louis when the exploit occured. The vents in the Jeep Cherokee started blasting cold air at the maximum setting; the radio switched to the local hip hop station; then the windshield wipers turned on, and wiper fluid blurred the glass. Next, the transmission was cut and the accelerator stopped working. Andy was alarmed and panic started to set in. Fortunately, this was a planned test, but one where the driver had no idea what type of attack would be launched. Greenberg was able to pull over safely.[3]

Hacking Joyride

Chrysler was able to quietly patch the vulnerability ahead of the Black Hat security conference in Las Vegas the following month. A black hat hacker is the most destructive in a group of hackers as they are malicious and pursue personal gain.[4] Not all hacking or malware seeks to gain personal information and trade secrets. I'm imagining some bored techie in a remote area who, instead of taking a revved up car out for a joy ride, is experimenting with malware, viruses, worms and other ploys to take control of vulnerable systems. A hacking joyride may be the extent of your downfall, but replacing corrupted code with healthy mental code and putting up layers of protection are your best defense.

A hacking joyride may be the extent ot your downfall,
but putting uplayers of protection are your best defense.

Our world is a different place than it was thirty, twenty, or even ten years ago, but you don't have to recoil in fear of every cyber vulnerability. However, the prudent use of available security tools to protect and defend both your property and your mind is a healthy mindset. If you keep circling around in a loop, with the same identical solutions that didn't work then and still don't work now, you may find yourself repeating and living through the same mistakes.

Snaked Chute

Since some of my immediate family milked cows while they were growing up, it's fun for me to read about natural animal behavior, especially for cattle. Temple Grandin, Ph.D. is an animal behavioral expert, with a specific focus on cattle. (If you are not familiar with Grandin's life, it is an interesting one as she has persevered through her autism to gain her education and expertise. In her work, she uses her visual memory to discover insights in the mind of cattle.)

According to Grandin, cattle have a natural tendency to circle around a handler in a pen, moving along the inner radius of the pen, not wanting to touch the edges. This makes it difficult to move the cattle out of the pen and into a chute designed to move them out for vaccinations or other procedures.[5] Therefore, Grandin suggests an entrance from the pen wide enough for several cows that slowly squeezes them into a single file in a curved, or snaked chute. As cattle naturally go where their nose is pointed, possessing wide angle vision,[6] the snaked chute is effective with less stimulus and distraction. They are now moving in what they feel is a safe or comfortable place, which is their natural instinct. This behavior is in response to pressure and their desire to remove pressure.[7]

Many people react similarly to cattle, rotating around a safe place, pointed where those have gone before. Breaking a habit or tendency like this in your life takes the insertion of a new path to squeeze you in a different direction. It may take a powerful tool, similar to a power saw, to carve a different path, even leading you down a curved, or snaked chute that will allow you to travel to healthy mental destinations.

Many people react similarly to cattle, rotating around a safe place, pointed where those have gone before.

Willingness to Change

Have you noticed that certain similar characteristics and mindsets are passed down from generation to generation, creating what seems like a never ending cycle? If you look at a family like the Kennedys, you see that many of the family have gone into politics, generation after generation. Also, many of the family faced tragedy and heartbreak, from the shooting of J.F.K. to the plane crash of John, Jr.

The Rockefeller family made one of the world's largest fortunes in the oil business during the late 19th and early 20th centuries. They are still known as one of the most powerful families in the history of the United States. One reason that history repeats itself is because mental code is handed down and codified within families.

Many habits work the same way, being cyclic. A caustic outlook may stem from a distinguishing attitude in a parent. Some are undermined by fear and inability to stay in a long term relationship because of the background of unstable family relationships, friendships or even abuse. There are others who face depression, anxiety and a number of other physical symptoms as inherited mental codes. A power saw has a toothed or abrasive blade to cut and grip different materials. It is a good picture of the strength it takes to cut through embedded mental code influenced by an interited, difficult past.

If a computer program can be tricked into writing data that is different than needed, your mind can also be tricked with faulty commands.

Unless a choice is made to use power tools to alter the vulnerabilities and cyclic bad code, the cycle will continue. Safeguarding yourself against malware of the mind with security updates and patches is a powerful mental tool. Moving around a different path than expected, even creating a snaked chute, will free you up from echoes of past repetition. It's a particularly powerful tool in breaking strongholds of inherited negative mental code.

 **TOOLS:**

A patch to exchange vulnerabilities with an executable or replaceable file; power saw to create a snaked chute to break strongholds and cyclic patterns in your life.

 MINDSETS:

• Take positive action with steady vigilance to own and control your thoughts. If your feelings are scrambled and confused, have a back-up plan for refocusing your mind with precision and confidence, inserting a new mental patch that will change your mental outlook.

• Recognize that your mind can be tricked with faulty commands, just as a computer.

• Identify some inherited characteristics of bad mental code that you can change. Accept the thoughts and actions you can't adjust now, but may in the future.

• Insert a patch of a constructive mindset or attitude to turn a standstill into positive movement for your business.

79

CHAPTER 14

MANAGEMENT TOOL: WEIGH and LEVERAGE

Managing risk is achievable as you perceptively weigh your options and leverage the outcome.

A scale in construction measures volume and weight. It determines the capacity of a load. Many times, in order to manage heavy objects, leverage is needed. A lever is a rigid bar with an end that can be placed beneath a heavy object to move or manage even a large piece of cement, rock or sewer pipe. Weighing options is one way to eliminate the bad code of unwise decisions. A lever provides the strength to make weighty changes that are needed.

Similarly, education acts as a lever for many, providing the ability to rise above generational circumstances. There are countless stories of first generation college students coming from a family that did not have the opportunity to receive a quality education. Rising above objections and ridicule, they chose to break the cycle, choosing to go down a "snaked chute," bumping and knocking against the the chute towards their education. This resulted in leveraging future possibilities with less exertion than previous generations.

Another value of weighing options is balancing risk vs. reward. This assessment helps in changing jobs, making dietary changes and leveraging education with a more accurate outcome.

Get Some Fresh Air

My father tells the story about how our extended family was saved because as an infant, I started screaming in the middle of the night. Apparently it was very cold and my parents, my grandmother and I were sleeping in a small room in Biloxi, Mississippi. Everyone was fast asleep when I started crying, hard. When my father got up to see what the problem was, he didn't feel quite right, a bit dizzy and off balance.

He immediately started opening all the windows, the door, and got everyone up and out of the house. He then turned off the small floor heater that was pouring out carbon monoxide. Without the alarming cries, we would have all kept sleeping, forever.

Often, fear or uncertainty can cause the same sense of dizziness. If so, it's time to open some windows to bring in fresh air and view your situation from a new perspective. This evaluation can come from wise counsel of a close friend or trusted family member. If fear and unhealthy conditions are fed by bad code, making you dizzy and off balance, step back and look at the entirety of the situation. After considering your circumstances with a clearer assessment, make the commitment to change now or you, too, may just keep sleeping, forever, for the rest of your life.

If you face fear or uncertainty about needed change,
it's time to view your situation from a new perspective.

Breakaway From Guilt

Linda Banks-Santilli, associate professor of education at Wheelock College, defines "breakaway guilt" as what many first generation college students face with their decision to pursue higher education, leaving their families behind. She was one of those students who felt as if she lived a double life. She had two identities, one for home and another for college.

Many face the same weighty feelings like Santilli did, as if they're abandoning parents or siblings who depend on them. Families may feel the student's desire for education and upward mobility is a rejection of their past. The good news is that with the right support and counsel, first generation students can leverage the weight of their past and go on to earn their degrees, reinvent themselves and reposition their families in positive ways for generations to come.[1]

Today, there is more help than ever available for those first generation students to help lift their emotional roadblocks. After Santilli faced her guilt by accurately weighing her situation, she finished her education. She then chose to give back by being a professional mentor. Guidance like Santilli's is available as an incredibly powerful tool that will provide the knowledge and strength to carve a new path without the heaviness of guilt. You just have to seek it out.

Howard Shultz, chairman and CEO of Starbucks Coffee, was a first generation college student, growing up in the Brooklyn, New York's federally subsidized housing projects. When leaving Brooklyn to go to college in Michigan, he was scared, insecure and didn't know anyone. Furthermore, those fears didn't go away after graduating college: fear of failure, of the unknown, of not finding success or of disappointing people. Still, Shultz managed his fear, keeping his core purpose in mind. Now he seeks to enhance the lives of those he is responsible for in his company.[2]

Do You Have Worms?

Some areas of life, such as emotional traits, are extremely difficult to change, nor are they solved with a quick fix of fresh air. It takes a firm decision, continuous action, and most often, outside help to forge a new course. Emotional instability is comparable to a computer virus that keeps replicating; unless appropriate measures are taken at the source, the resolution will not last or be effective.

Because the virus I found on my website acted as a worm, (a virus that is hiding, but when unleashed, spreads automatically), it had to be completely eliminated, so I hired professional outside help to fix the problem. The solution involved completely trashing my old theme files and inserting the patch of clean files.[3]

The definition of a physical virus is a microorganism that must attach itself to a living cell to reproduce. The fact that blog .php files are *dynamic,* living and changeable, as opposed to .html files that are *static,* staying the same, makes WordPress and blog pages prime targets to host computer viruses. In the same way, many areas of your life are *dynamic* and open to attack. Those areas may be easier to change than static areas, but they all take weighing decisions carefully, then taking affirmative defensive action.

Many areas of your life are dynamic and open to attack.

In a meeting with Dr. Tony Coulson, Ph.D., professor and director of Cyber Security Center at California State University, San Bernardino, he said, "The best way to add security and resist bad code is having a good defense."[4] To add a good defense costs money, time and definite effort and focus. A relevant example of appropriate defensive action that leverages survival rates pertains to breast cancer.

Defensive Action to Save Lives

The earlier breast cancer is found, the more likely the cancer will be eliminated. The most important weapon in the battle against breast cancer is the knowledge of family history of the disease. In fact, the risk is 1.8 times higher when a first degree relative (mother, sister, father or brother) has been diagnosed with the disease.[5]

With early diagnosis, especially Stage 0 and Stage 1, there is a 100% survival rate. The Stage 2 survival rate is 93%. When you know the risks, you can better weigh your options by further preparing yourself, getting the diagnosis and treatment you need.

Calculating your risks based on your family history helps you create a good defense, whether it's to fight cancer, an attitude, a habit or even negative self-talk.

The threat of a computer virus is always a risk if you have any online device. However, in the same way as breast cancer, you can leverage that risk and outcome with proper defensive action and education. With emotional viruses such as fear, depression and bitterness, honest evaluation is the first step to help manage and leverage their effect on your life.

Risk Management

If you didn't feel fear, you wouldn't protect yourself from legitimate threats. Fear is the feeling you get while standing on the precipice of a cliff, heart pounding and mind racing, deciding whether or not to dive into the waters below. I distinctly remember the feeling I had standing on the edge of a cliff, facing a jump into the Colorado River. My toes were curled over the edge, but as I weighed the risk, partially based on several memorable bellyflops, I backed off from the dubious pleasure. Then my younger sister stepped right up and immediately jumped.

Fortunately, she was fine, but I still felt tremendous fear watching her! Even though all turned out well, with many others jumping safely that day, the management of my fear identified and assessed the risk for me. I'm not sure my sister remembers her jump, but it was fortunate that no one was hurt. It was a popular place to jump and perhaps seemed much more daunting to me at the time, as one who is not fond of heights.

Some adventures hold more risk than others. If you have ever gone scuba diving, you realize accidents do happen. Advances in equipment design and proper training have brought the risk of recreational scuba diving slightly below the risks of horseback riding and golf and just above table tennis. Scuba diving is a prime example of how proper training can lower risk. [6]

Educating yourself, whether with a college education or in risk management, demonstrated by jumping off a cliff into a river below, incorporates good offense and defense. Most every profession, including the fields of medicine, finance and law require continuing education as it creates greater leverage. They all realize the great benefit of new and current information that influence life, wealth and freedoms. Continuing education, with a lifelong learner attitude, whether for a profession or developing positive self-talk, will help you leverage and manage the current offensive and defensive mental tools with an open mind for your life and future.

 **TOOLS:**

Scale to weigh your options and manage risk; bar to leverage future opportunities with lifelong learning.

 MINDSETS:

• Visually open some windows to face fear or uncertainty about what needs to change. Doing so will give you the feeling of fresh air and possibly a new perspective.

• Honestly evaluate emotional viruses as fear, depression and bitterness. That assessment is a healthy first step to help you weigh and leverage their effect on your life. Seek help from a close friend or trusted family member to help you evaluate and provide a different perspective.

• Define some areas of continuing education for your life, incorporating a lifelong learner attitude. Whether for a profession, business or developing positive self-talk, the skills you learn and maintain will help you leverage and manage the current offensive and defensive tools for your life and future.

CHAPTER 15

PERSONAL TOOL:
ORGANIZE and GAUGE PRESSURE

A blowout may occur when there is unseen pressure
acting as an undercurrent of stress that is not
immediately visible from the outside.

I've always loved my dad's homemade rustic, heavy toolbox. The worn printing on the outside says "Ye Old Toolbox." My dad always emphasized, "Get your tools ready the night before." He knew firsthand that having your tools assembled saved not only time, but a great deal of effort and money when he had workers show up to work early the next morning.

His advice has proved tremendously effective in many areas of my life, whether in preparing music charts for a studio session or finishing a home improvement project. My husband and I recently found that having the appropriate tools made a huge difference in assembling a closet organizer, a task stressful enough to break up many a marriage!

In addition, a good tire gauge comes in handy when hauling the larger tools of life. It serves as a good example of how helpful it is to test pressure in our lives. Both a sturdy toolbox with a durable handle and a pressure gauge are helpful in developing good mental code.

How Sturdy is Your Toolbox?

It may be chipped and worn, but your toolbox doesn't need to be pretty to be functional. It will provide you with the tools you need to make important changes. However, as I learned from my father, it should have a strong handle and a fair amount of durability. Inside that toolbox one of the most used, yet appreciated tools, is a pressure gauge. This gauge is used to ensure that daily loads can be transferred safely and smoothly.

A sturdy toolbox with a durable handle and a pressure gauge are vital daily tools to develop and maintain good mental code.

Even though my father's toolbox was not huge, it was adequate to handle the tools he needed. It weathered storms, falling off the back of a truck and held its share of neglected tools lodged in the crevices. Many wait for just the right solution or fancy tool to come bouncing out of their toolbox before they attempt to change their mental code and outlook. They keep delaying action but don't realize looks are many times deceiving. Often, the ordinary solution may be readily available and effective in bringing a solution to a problem and doesn't need a psychologist to analyze and prescribe a remedy.

Hidden Pressures

As there are some pressures that create weakness and unseen tears in the linings of a tire, there can also be stress in the linings of our life and even immune system. Part of what I do professionally is perform as a pianist and vocalist for large auditorium audiences. In order to travel quickly and effectively, I keep a trailer on our property with show gear inside. For a recent tour, I decided to pull out my pressure gauge to make sure the tires, after sitting in the hot sun during some recent hot weather, could handle the load for the trip. The gauge found my tires to be holding the air effectively. The tire store also confirmed the tires were fine for the trip, so we went off on our tour.

On the way back from the tour, traveling on a two-lane highway, I heard and felt a loud jolt and knocking noise associated with a blowout. Slowly moving over to the roadside, my fears were confirmed with the outside tread of one of the tires completely torn off. When checked before the trip, the tires held the correct pressure, but there were other unseen problems being created by stress on the inside. Fortunately, I was able to drive slowly, mostly on the soft shoulder of the road, to the next small town with one small shop that miraculously had a tire we needed. The blowout occured with the unseen pressure not immediately visible from the outside. Some physical viruses act the same way.

The Correct Diagnosis

A little over a year ago, I started experiencing severe headaches not even two prescribed Vicodin tablets could dull. After a number of online searches, I was fairly certain I had a brain tumor, but I decided not to panic and see a doctor. After my regular MD couldn't find anything, I went to the eye doctor, for by this point I could barely open my left eye.

After several appointments and a breakout of a rash on my forehead and left eyelid, the eye doctor diagnosed my condition: a severe case of shingles affecting my left eye. In hindsight, I realize I could have lost that eye without the correct diagnosis and treatment.

I knew little about about shingles before this time and thought it was only for old people beyond 80, of which I'm not close! Apparently this is not the case, as it can occur at a much younger age. Even though shingles is a virus, similar to the chicken pox, many say the onset can be triggered by the long-term wear of stress prompting a blowout, just like a tire.

An unhealthy view of self and stress can attack just as fiercely
as shingles, crippling and paralyzing you.

Stress Points

Though stress is not a proven single cause of shingles, I still took a good look at my pressure gauge. I started questioning if I was guarding my emotions, holding them in. Were my feelings about to burst like a tire too full of pressure, or did I have a healthy outlet of vulnerability?

Lying flat on your back for weeks, even months as I was, gives you the chance to ponder situations you normally wouldn't consider. Just as the shingles virus attacked my body, an unhealthy view of self and long term stress can attack just as fiercely, crippling and paralyzing you. You may even lose your ability to see!

A core area of anxiety and stress for many is a healthy self image. A negative self view of bad code can act like a slow leak, just as oil leaking from an engine or air from a tire. It's a good exercise to reflect on how you feel about you. Do you question your ability to add value to relationships or to situations? Self confidence comes from not only recognizing, but also trusting in your abilities, qualities and judgment.

A negative self view of bad code can act like a slow leak, just as oil leaking from an engine or air from a tire.

Bottled Up Emotions

If you are feeling guilt, shame or personal depression, you may be evaluating your worthiness by what others think or feel about you. With a negative evaluation comes the fear to take risks, the fear to fail, the fear to be who you really are. This statement by Brené Brown, a self-proclaimed shame researcher, is one of my favorites: "Only when we're brave enough to explore the darkness will we discover the infinite power of our light."[1]

Shame and self-doubt encourage the onslaught of stress, depression and even a "victim mentality." Expressing those feelings honestly, then working through them will help you to confront and reduce the pressure that stress brings. A few good and trusted friends or counselors in your life are priceless gifts, as they can help you put life in perspective. Also disciplines like prayer, light exercise and small breaks to walk outside and enjoy the pallet of colors, sights and sounds around you help you handle a daily load in a healthy way.

Equivalent to stress is emotional weight or heaviness. I have felt heaviness many times where I've swallowed my emotions to play piano and sing for tough funerals. Memorial services for children whose lives were snuffed out much too soon: some for boys my sons' ages, who never were able to experience homecoming or prom. There were other instances of holding back tears of joy, singing for a friend's wedding: a special friend who thought she'd never feel love again.

Disciplines like prayer, light exercise and small breaks to walk outside and enjoy the pallet of colors, sights and sounds around you help you handle a daily load in a healthy way.

There's a balance of controlling feelings when you are an entertainer, but also a time for showing emotion. As years passed, I found my shell of protection stayed on and it was difficult to let loose of the guardedness I felt. It became difficult to really feel compassion, even to weep. I tended to bottle it up inside in a protective carafe, ready to burst.

Maybe you, too, have put a tight armor of protection around your emotions. The danger comes with not ever taking that armor off, seldom exposing yourself to the light of vulnerability. As time passes, if the armor stays on, guarded protectiveness becomes a habit and results in the negative code of defensiveness, stress and even illness. Many books and self help guides tout a solution of positive thinking for anxiety, but that alone is insufficient. For an honest evaluation, you may need to emotionally shed that protective shell and apply an accurate gauge of assessment with good counsel and coaching.

If the armor stays on, guarded protectiveness becomes a habit and results in the negative code of defensiveness, stress and even illness.

Positive Self-Talk

Even if I wanted to become a ballerina, no amount of positive thinking or optimistic attitude would get me there. Why? Because I can't even touch my toes! I could make up enough colorful visual boards to fill a room with famous dancers and inspirational sayings, but becoming a ballerina is not a realistic goal for my body type. There have been numerous great books written on positive thinking and the power of positive thinking. However, there are many things in life that won't be accomplished by mere positive thinking.

If a simple Band-Aid is put on a hemorrhaging wound, the bleeding may slow down, but not stop. A more permanent solution is evaluating, defining and dealing with the source of the injury, even if it involves surgery or stitches. Pain usually acts as a gauge for the severity of the injury. A broken foot creates a great deal of pain, demanding a different remedy than a turned ankle. This principle often holds true in measuring the intensity of stress when evaluating and defining the source of the problem.

For an honest evaluation, you may need to emotionally shed that protective shell and apply an accurate gauge of assessment with good counsel and coaching.

Where You Let Your Mind Reside

Whatever your personal belief, there are some great points of guidance that are in the Holy Scriptures. In the New Testament book of Philippians, written approximately 61 A.D. by the Apostle Paul, Paul focuses on positive steps of thankfulness and encouragement. As a zealous Jewish leader, he had plenty of events in his life for which he could carry guilt. Paul could have beat himself up emotionally for years, as he persecuted and executed many innocent Christians before his life-changing experience with a blinding light on the road to Damascus.

Paul said, "If there is any excellence and if anything worthy of praise, dwell on these things." (Philippians 4:8)[2] To "dwell" means to "live in." To "live in" means to reside. In other words, let your mind reside on aspects in your life that are worthy of admiration and approval. When you let something in your life, you are making the decision to open up the gate. Just as cattle tend to go to the last known comfortable place, humans mentally go to the place that is easiest to access.

No matter how chipped and worn, your mental toolbox
will serve you well through all your days.

For enduring and lasting change of negative self-talk and the mental pressure of a victim mentality, choosing to stay in a dark mental place of anger and hopelessness, a sturdy toolbox is valuable and necessary. The level of your pressure gauge may change throughout the decades of your life as the tread of your life wears thin with new challenges. However, no matter how chipped and worn, your mental toolbox will serve you well.

 **TOOLS:**

Sturdy Toolbox to carry the weight of your tools; gauge to analyze and measure pressure in your life.

 MINDSETS:

• Create your own personal mental toolbox, including a gauge, to help you determine and measure pressure. This will help you in developing good mental code.
• Determine and shed any emotional guarded shell you are wearing and apply an accurate and honest gauge of assessment with honest counsel and coaching.
• Let your mind reside on the good things in life, as the Apostle Paul spoke of. It will help you begin the journey down the snaked chute that acts as a power tool for real transformation.
• Take on the disciplines like prayer, light exercise and small breaks to walk outside and enjoy the pallet of colors, sights and sounds to help handle daily stress.

Ye Old Toolbox

CHAPTER 16

POSITIVE TOOL:
BLESSED LIST and LAUGHTER

*Your blessed list and ability to laugh are wonderful positive tools
you should always keep in your mental toolbox.*

I have the habit of saving every little nut and bolt I find as I think I
may need it someday! As a result, I have small bags of miscellaneous
items containing an assortment of objects in all different sizes in our
garage. The truth is, I will seldom or never use those items; however,
recently those bags full of goodies came in handy, along with a good
screwdriver.

My husband and I were hanging some mirrors in our
remodeled bathrooms, and the task required larger drywall sinkers
than the ones provided. I found those items in our garage, in a small,
organized bag. Further, I decided to hang a few new pictures in our
bedroom and again, found just the right small nails in our garage,
in a small container. Just as saving the right miscellaneous screws
may someday save you a lot of time during a home repair project,
obtaining the right positive tools in your personal development
box will save you a lot of time and emotional energy. Picture a
screwdriver as symbolizing the turning of negative self-talk to a
positive, constructive attitude; then pair it with the nuts and bolts of
a blessed list and a good laugh.

Your Blessed List

You may not actually be physically hanging mirrors or pictures, but possessing the right array of tools to protect against unexpected attacks of discouragement, stress, unhealthy fear or anger will save you much emotional energy. Developing your blessed list, looking for the humor in life and shedding the heavy vest of unhealthy seriousness are great additions to include in your mental of toolbox because a positive mental outlook can even prevent symptoms of aging.

Possessing the right tools to protect against a number of unexpected attacks will save you much emotional energy.

Once, we moved a family member into a local, wonderful brand new senior facility that provided constant activities, care and a beautiful place to live. However, she returned to her former home situation after just three weeks. At home, she still received full time care, but with none of the delightful activities the facility offered. We moved her back to her familiar environment because the adjustment and change were too difficult for her.

Even though she communicated outward openness and willingness to move, her negative self-talk and the resulting fear she experienced overwhelmed her. You don't have to be ready for a retirement or care facility to experience those same feelings of panic and negativity. The inability to have balanced, positive self-talk can absolutely paralyze you, which prevents you from making adjustments, both personally and professionally. There is the fear of the unknown, focus on the past instead of the present, difficulty in developing new relationships and many times a drop in mental astuteness. For our dear relative, I believe a stronger focus on her blessed list would have helped her through the transition. A blessed list acts as a warm mineral spring, bubbling with a source of healing and gratitude when encountering difficult situations. However, you have to choose to think positively on a consistent basis.

Simple Pleasures

How do you develop the ability to sustain positive self-talk that even the Apostle Paul talked about? The first step is the mindset of thankfulness. Focus on simple pleasures with a blessed list several times a day; then repeat. Those simple pleasures can include the smell of morning coffee, the majesty of the mountains, a simple rose on a desk, or a computer that saves you time—at least occasionally! As Aristotle said, "We are what we repeatedly do. Excellence, then, is not an act, but a habit."[1] Make a habit of focusing on the simple pleasures.

Philip Simmons had Lou Gehrig's disease, diagnosed in 1993. He died in 2002, nine years later at the age of forty-five. He said in his book *Learning to Fall*:

> Each day that I can get out of bed in the morning, I am blessed. Each day that any of us can move our limbs to do the world's work, we are blessed. And if limbs wither, and speech fails, we are still blessed. So long as this heart beats, I am blessed, for it is our human work, it is our human duty, finally, to rise each day in the face of loss, to rise in the face of grief, of debility, of pain, to move as the turtle moves, her empty nest behind her, her labor come to nothing, up out of the pit and toward the next season's doing.[2]

Philip Simmons wrote those words in 2002, nine years after his diagnosis of ALS. Even though he was dying, he wrote about living despite, "...a degenerative illness bent on emptying me out one teaspoon at a time." Make your own personalized blessed list for every area of your life listing each area you can imagine where you are blessed. Then every day you get out of bed, review your blessed list with a grateful heart, repeating it over and over again. This is the first step in combatting the mental negative code that can easily overtake your life.

Make your own personalized blessed list for every area of your life listing each area you can imagine where you are blessed.

Laugher, the Best Medicine

I've always loved reading the *Readers Digest*[3] section "Laughter, The Best Medicine." It's a well documented fact that laughter brings on good vibes with endorphins that can heal the body and relieve stress. The positive health benefits are numerous when I exert a gut wrenching laugh.

Recently, I signed up for a Comedy Improv class with a friend of mine. I was quite nervous the first week as the mere idea of speaking without the safety net of a script or plan scared me to death, especially with comedy. Ask me to play anything on the piano, and I can make it up on the spot, but improv in speaking? That's a different story!

What I experienced was laugh after laugh. In fact, once in the middle of an impromptu sketch, I couldn't gain composure. I had tears running down my cheeks because the scene was so funny. As a result, I could not take myself seriously or think about how I looked. My mascara smeared from watery eyes as I blew my nose again and again, but at that point, I didn't care! Just like the purpose of a screwdriver is to turn a screw, so laughter can totally change your mental perspective from negative to positive when you let yourself see the humor in a situation.

The Scripted Life

There is a delicate balance between scripting life, which requires holding back emotions and thoughts, contrasted with unscripted reactions where a person completely loses control of a situation, not knowing where it will take her. When you are in good physical shape, your heart rate returns to normal more quickly after an intense cardio workout. In a similar way, putting yourself in improvisational situations can increase your emotional stamina, allowing you to gain composure much faster. I hope to gain much stamina in my improv class, but I definitely don't want to stop the laughter—it's fun and I need it!

Funny stories are all around you. Despite all the tragic events reported on the news, there are little nuggets of humorous stories that can make you giggle. For instance, there was a suspected bank robber who was arrested twenty minutes after the robbery while eating chicken and biscuits. Apparently, he worked up an appetite robbing the Citizens Bank in New Kensington, Pennsylvania and ran by a restaurant just two blocks away. He realized he was hungry, turned back and went inside. Police arrested the man while he sat at a booth, devouring his food along with the other customers. I guess he should have eaten earlier![4] You just can't make this stuff up.

Humor acts like a weighted vest, allowing you to shed the heaviness depression brings.

Shed That Vest

One of our sons, when training for the Fire Academy, wore a weighted vest while running. Afterward, taking the heavy vest off gave him a feeling of freedom and relief and actually helped him increase his running speed.

Humor acts like a weighted vest, allowing you to shed the heaviness depression brings. Even Scott Hamilton, 1984 Olympic gold medalist for figure skating said, "I've noticed that people who laugh are healthier than people who feel stressed."[5] Hamilton himself overcame many physical challenges, including a mysterious illness that caused him to stop growing, a bout with testicular cancer and a brain tumor.

Brevity and humor can diffuse arguments, lift the gloom in a room and even provide physical healing. Laughter can turn a dark thundercloud to pinpricks of lambent light peeking through the sky. There is definitely a place for seriousness, focus, concentration and winning. However, shame, discouragement and negativity can act as heavy weights, similar to a weighted vest. This extra bulk of negativity will only get heavier with increased stress and escalating years of life, where you feel your choices narrow to a small puncture of influence. Just like the dwarfs in the Brothers Grimm fairy tale *Snow*

White[6], your focus will determine whether you are named Grumpy or Happy. Your blessed list can be a natural hot spring, overflowing with the bubbling warmth of refreshment and joy, which is the true source of happiness. Having joy and ability to laugh are wonderful positive tools you should always keep in your toolbox.

 **TOOLS:**

A screwdriver typifies how a blessed list has the ability to turn negative thoughts to a positive attitude; nuts and bolts illustrate how adding laughter and bits of humor lighten the weight of shame, discouragement and negativity.

 MINDSETS:

• Develop your blessed list; look for the funny, and shed the weighted vest of unhealthy seriousness. They are great additions to include in your mental toolbox as they can lift the gloom in a room and in some situations, provide physical healing.

• Make your own personalized blessed list. Identify every area of your life, listing every thing you can imagine where you are blessed. Your blessed list will act as a natural hot spring, overflowing with the bubbling warmth of refreshment and joy, which is the true source of happiness.

• Realize the purpose of a weighted vest is to make you stronger. However, if that vest holds shame, discouragement and negativity and is not shed, it is destructive. Identify and eliminate the mental thoughts that are weighing you down. Replace them with a new perspective supported by items on your blessed list or humor.

Ye Old Toolbox

CHAPTER 17

SHAPING TOOL:
SELF-EFFACEMENT and REFINING

Diffusing an intense situation takes a clear focus and thick skin.
Use multiple tools to emphasize what truly matters.

The Kailash Temple in Ellora, India is one of the largest Hindu temples in the world. It is a megalith, carved out of one single rock, notable for its vertical excavation, formed from the top downward. It is estimated that between 150 and 300 men worked on it at one time, working from the summit with their hammers and chisels to create an amazing structure.

Started in the mid-eighth century and probably taking about 100 years to complete, the impressive structure is twice the area of Greece's Parthenon and fifty percent taller.[1] The amount of rock that had to be hand carved with chisel and hammer is astounding, considering the work it took to create both smooth and ornate surfaces. In the same way, the example of a good chisel wielded correctly will help you develop a slick back to repel flaming arrows of criticism. Also, just as a hammer and chisel combined will change the shape of a large rock, you can change the shape of your life by chipping away at the toughness formed from stubbornness and pride.

Thick Skin

The rhinoceros has tough, leathery skin, roughly 1.5 centimeters thick, which is a little over a half inch. The armadillo has a hard outer shell and additional armor that covers the top of its head, limbs, and tail. However its underside consists of soft skin and fur. The walrus has hardy, wrinkled skin up to four centimeters thick, which is equivalent to over one and a half inches.

Human skin is much thinner, two to three millimeters thick, which is about a tenth of an inch. Skin is the largest organ in the human body with a surface area of sixteen to twenty-one square feet. As skin ages, it becomes thinner and is easily damaged. However, there are occasions where it is beneficial to develop a "thicker skin" when it comes to criticism.

Life holds many opportunities for criticism, some of it constructive and productive, and some of it negative and damaging. Humans would have a difficult time moving if they literally had skin the thickness of rhinoceros or walrus skin. However, as demonstrated with the introduction of reality shows, participants must develop a thick skin. There are many instances where the featured subjects don't just laugh. They have to let insults or jeers roll off and not take themselves too seriously.

Life holds many opportunities for criticism, some of it constructive and productive and some of it negative and damaging.

Reality Sells

Allen Funt, with his 1948 T.V. series *Candid Camera* is often credited as the creator of reality T.V. There were secret cameras to record people in unexpected circumstances. I remember watching an episode on late night T.V., in black and white, with a person receiving a call on a local pay phone. When the caller sneezed, water came out of the phone handle and the recipient's look of surprise and disgust was hilarious. Reality shows have increased in popularity, selling more than ever. A well-known current show is *Keeping Up with the Kardashians*.

The Kardashian show has consistently received poor reviews from critics who deplore the focus on the "famous for being famous" concept. Several critics also describe the family as "self absorbed" and "desperate" for fame. Whatever your opinion, the long running reality series mirrors much of our society's wants, hopes and dreams.

Apparently the wide viewership audience loves to follow the story lines and drama, even if such scenes are often fabricated. The Kardashians, or any other reality show personalities, can't take themselves too seriously if they are to show what's "real." Even though the Kardashians promote their self absorbed celebrity, they seem undeterred by undesirable reviews. Maybe they read Eleanor Roosevelt's words.

Rhinoceros Hide

Eleanor offered this timeless advice to women working in politics in 1936: "You cannot take anything personally, you cannot bear grudges. You cannot get discouraged too easily." Above all, Eleanor insisted, "[Every political woman needs] to develop skin as tough as rhinoceros hide!"[2]

To develop leathery skin has proven throughout history to be wise advice. If you follow any political campaign, with men or women running, remember that phrase. If there is political dirt to be dug up, it will surface. If there are relationships gone wrong, they will reveal themselves, many times with exaggerated and embellished statements. And what about the unflattering photos you see plastered on the gossip magazines, visibly displayed on most every newsstand? Not for the feint of heart!

Chip away on your own flaws and imperfections to create a back smooth enough to let biting and hurtful comments roll off.

Brené Brown in *Daring Greatly* said, "Nothing has transformed my life more than realizing that it's a waste of time to evaluate my worthiness by weighing the reaction of the people in the stands. The people who love me and will be there regardless of the outcome are within arm's reach."[3] Apparently the Kardashians have also taken those words to heart in creating their hit series! It is tempting to wallow in the stubbornness of self-pity that comes from hurtful remarks or judgmental quips. However, when you are able to gently chip away on your own flaws and imperfections, your back will be smooth enough to let biting and hurtful comments roll off. So much of your ability to do this boils down to your attitude and focus.

Shaping Your Attitude

I remember clearly the first time I played the board game *Risk* with my husband's family. If you've ever played, you know the object of the game is to take over the world. As I tend to be very competitive in any sort of game, I got intensely involved and focused and won. My victory did not go over very well with my late father-in-law who was a brilliant man and had played the game many times, also intending to win.

I immediately had to blame my winning on pure beginner's luck and quickly brought up a few stories where I had failed miserably, such as in playing golf, with self effacing humor. To be honest, inside I was jumping up and down, delighted by my own temerity in winning, but after quickly reminding myself that it was just a game, I changed my response. It reminded me of Plato's quote, "You can discover more about a person in an hour of play than in a year of conversation."[4] Realizing the relationship with my father-in-law was more important than my string of surprise successes prompted me to take a step back from my prideful gloating. I gained a new focus.

Playing down a short term victory will have long term benefits with a shift of emphasis, shaping your response for what truly matters.

102

Shaping Your Focus

Once, after working for a good hour at my local coffee shop, my laptop screen suddenly became blurry. I was quite concerned and took off my reading glasses, worried that my eyes could be fatigued, or worse. I found that my pair of multi-pack Costco reading glasses was missing a lens. I was relieved to discover the simple cause of my distorted vision! Once I realized the problem, I clarified my focus with a better pair of glasses, containing both lenses. In the same way, a slanted view of a situation or yourself can come from a distorted view and unclear focus.

You may never aim to have a reality show, but you will certainly find yourself in the situation where you have to make the decision to shape your attitude and response, using your hammer and chisel to carve through the rock of stubbornness and pride. Diffusing a situation that is intense takes a clear focus and thick skin, using multiple tools to shape your emphasis on what truly matters.

 **TOOLS:**

Hammer and chisel: to carve through the rock of stubbornness resulting from lack of self-evaluation or clear focus; also to develop a slick surface of self-effacement with a chisel's refinement.

 MINDSETS:

• Determine an area where developing thick leathery skin will help you weather a particularly touchy situation.

• Note what really matters in your life to keep a healthy perspective and focus. This helps not to alienate those people who have not developed a healthy point of view by reveling in your personal successes.

• Determine a short term victory that you can play down with the effect of a long term benefit. Use a shift of your emphasis, shaping your response for what truly matters.

• Chip away on your own flaws and imperfections for a back that will be smooth enough to let biting and hurtful comments roll off.

103

CHAPTER 18

FOCUSING TOOL:
DISCARD and SIMPLIFY

If your life is to be pithy and memorable, it takes eliminating what isn't needed and concentrating on what's extraordinary.

In Marie Kondo's life-changing book, *The Life Changing Magic of Tidying Up*, she emphasizes the importance of choosing what to keep, not what to get rid of. According to Kondo, you should, "Keep only those things that speak to your heart. Take the plunge and discard all the rest. By doing this, you can reset your life and embark on a new lifestyle."[1]

The reset button restarts the game in video game consoles. On computers, the reset button clears the memory and reboots the machine. To reset your life is not quite so simple as pushing a button, but Kondo gives good ideas on how to begin by bringing order to your surroundings. Getting rid of the excess is similar to filling multiple trash bags, many times at capacity.

Similarly, in a construction project, a sponge is used to wipe away extra cement or grout in a home-improvement project. A sponge is a good example of clearing off the unnecessary as Hans Hofmann, the influential German painter said so eloquently, "The ability to simplify means to eliminate the unnecessary so the necessary may speak."[2]

What's in Your Closet?

We recently survived a remodel, covering about half of our home, it was unexpected and unanticipated but necessary. It felt like moving as we cleared out rooms, closets and bathrooms. I'd love to say what an organized process this was, but that would be far from the truth. We not only filled up multiple trash cans, but also numerous dumpsters.

It is somewhat embarrassing to reveal what I found in closed drawers and closets. Old hair dye our sons had used in high school, when bleaching hair white was popular; a dozen empty deodorant containers; enough dental floss to last the next ten years; useless razors, both used and unused along with plenty of miscellaneous items.

My explorations into the deep recesses of our home reminded me of that popular T.V. show, *American Pickers*, where Mike Wolfe and Frank Fritz travel the U.S. to look for rare artifacts and national treasures. They explore people's homes, barns, sheds and other places. Some of those people are collectors, some are hoarders and some have inherited their Aunt Thelma's antiques.

American Pickers is fascinating to watch as it demonstrates how much "stuff" people keep. Americans live in a society where people have cars they don't drive parked in huge, spotless unused garages or clothes they don't wear, many still with tags attached, stuffed in multiple closets or storage facilities full of items they don't use now and possibly will never use again.

Discard to Retain

My husband and I run our businesses from home offices. I am finding it is becoming increasingly important, although difficult, to simplify our surroundings. Even with computers, it doesn't take long for stacks of papers and magazines to grow a foot high. As I dispose of mounds of material, my concentration becomes more clear and focused with less clutter. It takes a concerted, deliberate effort to repeatedly move stacks into the recycle bin along with "stuff" I think

I might need, read or enjoy later.

Some reading this may have aging parents. This should cause you to seriously evaluate your belongings, knowing someday you will go through your parents "stuff" and your kids will have to go through your "stuff." Kondo says, "To truly cherish the things that are important to you, you must first discard those that have outlived their purpose."[3] It is easy to feel guilt for discarding or passing along clothes, giving away so-called family heirlooms or even throwing away old photos. For some, this purging is extremely difficult and in certain cases, it's wise to bring in a professional organizer to help gain perspective and targeted help. ShopSmart, a division of *Consumer Reports,* reported in 2010 that most women own seven pair of jeans but only wear four pairs (if that!) on a regular basis.[4] Such surplus in many closets has not changed since then.

One of the great benefits of donating goods to organizations such as *Goodwill* or the *Salvation Army* is the good feeling you get when you think you are helping others with your "valuable stuff." In fact, Goodwill tries to recycle or send even unusable items to a salvage stream-textile or other type of recycler.[5] That bit of information actually makes me feel better about some of the bags I have personally left at their donation center with suspect items from our household.

> *In certain cases, it's wise to bring in a professional organizer to help gain perspective and targeted help.*

The Rose in the Room

Do a little self-test. When you walk in a room, what is the first thing you see? Too much clutter in a room means you can't focus on the beauty there, even if it's a single rose. Ridding a space of clutter is particularly helpful for creative people, like me, allowing for greater concentration, focus and effective work.

> *If there is too much clutter in a room, you can't focus on the beauty of what's there, even if it's a single rose.*

Even fine porcelain objects go through a process of scraping and sponging to rid the pieces of excess seams and clay, letting the true beauty of the figurine come through. My mother was involved in porcelain and ceramics, making intricate *Lladró* figurines as well as other antique reproductions. My sisters and I started making ugly mugs for our teachers in our middle school years as we experimented with multi-colored glaze, but gradually we improved our craft. In creating a piece of fine china, slip is poured into a mold; then every piece is cleaned with a small utility knife and wet sponge to smooth the edges. Because every piece of fine porcelain shrinks at least 15% in a first hot fire of nearly 1,000 degrees Celsius, cleaning off the excess with a scraper and sponge during the first steps of development is very important to preserve the fine detail of the piece. The same principle applies to life in cleaning off the excess clutter that can fill your mind, distracting you from clear and focused goals.

Elaine St. James, in *Living the Simple Life*, said she probably would have simplified her life sooner if she knew she could spend her new found time facing the more difficult challenges she'd spent years avoiding, such as conquering her fears or learning to forgive.[6] There's no quick and easy formula to simplifying and "sponging off" the excess. Such junk manifests itself in a little different way for everyone.

Pithy Principle

One of the most difficult steps in writing books, songs, musicals or even comedy is eliminating what is not really needed. Making every word and thought count is the goal of good writing. The definition of "pithy" is "concise and forcefully expressive." I readily admit that I had to look the word up the first time I heard the term.

To be pithy is to use few words in a clever, effective way. A pithy phrase or melody is one you walk away repeating or singing. It's memorable, has a hook, is concise and to the point.

Twitter is a prime example of a platform for pithy phrases, enforced by the limit of 140 characters.

To make life pithy and memorable requires eliminating what isn't needed and concentrating on what's extraordinary. That is a huge challenge not only for a creative writer, but for every person who desires to do their best work and live a full and productive life through the decades.

> *Like sponging off the excess seams from a fine piece of porcelain, removing the superfluous will help you focus on the essential and beautiful things in life.*

Gabriel's Angels

Pam Gaber led the Veterinary and Pet Divisions for Sandoz Pharmaceutical in the U.S. but at one point, she realized she didn't have a life outside of work. She was constantly flying around the country, seldom taking a day off. She made the tough call to exit corporate America, changing her life and quitting her job. After six months, she adopted a Weimaraner puppy. Pam never set out to change the world, but she and the story of her dog inspired a revolution.

Pam and her dog started *Gabriel's Angels*, an organization that visits and serves 13,700 abused, neglected, and at risk children in the Phoenix and Tucson, Arizona areas. Its mission is to deliver healing pet therapy, nurturing the children's emotional development and enhancing the quality of their lives forever. At this point, they have nearly 175 registered volunteer therapy teams and 40 helping hands delivering pet therapy to over 100 agencies.[7]

Eliminate and Concentrate

If Pam had not eliminated her high pressure job and made a change to simplify her life, she never would have adopted a dog that started a whole movement. Just as a low lying fog can keep you from seeing the vehicle in front of you, clutter and busyness can distort and cloud your sense of purpose and happiness. It's very difficult for some to move, discard and change. However, just like sponging off the excess seams from a fine piece of porcelain, removing the superfluous will help you focus on the essential and beautiful things in life.

Try eliminating one thing; live with the results; then remove something else. Fairly soon, you will have room to move and your mind will have room to think where you had no room before. Mentally eliminate distracting thoughts with sturdy trash bags and clean the edges of your life with a sponge to see the fine detail. You will then be on the road to tidier, clearer concentration for good, pithy mental code.

 **TOOLS:**

Trash bags to eliminate the excess clutter that will fill your mind and space; sponge to clear off the excess and see the fine detail in life.

 MINDSETS:

• Make a detailed list of what you can shed and discard to help you see the beauty around you.

• Reaffirm that getting rid of clutter particularly helps creative people concentrate with greater focus and work more effectively.

• As you eliminate what isn't needed, think in *Twitter Tweets* to concentrate on the extraordinary. Remove the unnecessary to see the necessary.

• Eliminate, then concentrate and you will be on the road to tidy up and reset your life with good, pithy mental code.

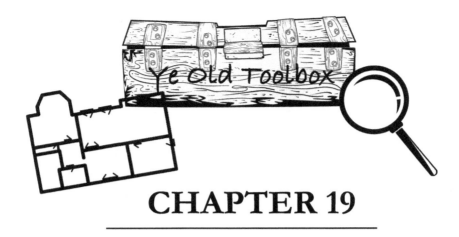

CHAPTER 19

REFACTORING TOOL: EXAMINE and PLAN

You may find smelly mental code in the form of attitudes or emotions that are causing a mental fungus that can stink up your life.

A magnifying glass lets you see an enlarged image. It is helpful when one is experiencing declining eyesight. In the same way, examining code takes some sort of magnification. The principle of refactoring on a computer is a good place to begin for inspecting and modifying code, as many times it involves simplifying and increasing the readability and understanding of existing code that needs modification. To refactor is to "restructure or rearrange." If you change the structure of a building, you need a good set of plans for a remodel. The same holds true in restructuring code.

To gain access to code and make changes, you need to be named as an administrator with a current username and password. It's not too difficult or complicated to simply rearrange or change the structure of the code. However, changing bad mental code into new, healthy good code is much more involved than just gaining access and changing a password; however, doing so will start the process along with magnified examination to develop a workable plan.

Restructuring Principle

The principle of refactoring in computer code is the procedure of restructuring existing computer code without changing the external behavior. The advantages include improved readability and code complexity.[1] For example, two bathrooms in our home served the same purpose both before and after a major remodel--they were bathrooms. However, when we observed warped drywall in several places, we knew there was a deep problem with internal plumbing that required updating and changing the bathrooms. If we failed to correct the leaks, the problem would remain and worsen over time. The external purpose of our bathrooms stayed the same, but the internal parts changed when we corrected the problems.

In applying the refactoring principle to your life, it works much the same way as our bathroom repair and remodel. If you want lasting changes from refactoring bad mental code and finding ways to create good mental code, you need to go much farther than tweaking the outward appearance of your code. You need to look at the foundation of the problem, viewing it under magnification. Recognizing what is unhealthy and then changing to something that is strong and vigorous takes positive and purposeful action to transform what is within. It takes going to the source files where you may find smelly code.

Recognizing what is unhealthy and then changing it to something that is strong and vigorous takes positive and purposeful action to transform what is within.

Smelly Code

Smelly Code, also known as bad smell in computer programming code, refers to any symptom indicating a deeper problem.[2] I often see skunks in our neighborhood but so far have been successful in avoiding them. Others have not been so fortunate, however, especially some of the pets, both large and small, that seem to think they can overtake the black and white mound of slow-moving fur.

They, as well as their owners, are greeted with a smelly surprise. Neutralizing skunk odor requires a great deal of effort, including the right concoction of juices and sprays to clean up the oily, malodorous mess that has remarkable lingering power. Unlike skunks, you can't physically sniff out smelly code when it's on your computer, but it can lurk beneath the surface and stink just as potently as a lingering skunk stench.

Just as smelly code helps to identify problems in the virtual world on a computer, there is smelly code in your personal and professional life that will help you identify areas that can be revised and changed, helping you transform bad mental code to good mental code. Unlike a broken water pipe or plumbing in a bathroom, most bad smells affecting computer code have been present since its creation.

In the same way, you, too, may feel that you have been born with some of the bad code you are presently facing. How often have you heard the familiar words, "I was born this way," or "This is just the way I am"? If you are not careful, those words become excuses never to change, so the smell of skunk will never go away.

There is smelly code in your personal and professional life that will help you identify areas that can be revised and changed.

Emperor's New Clothes

I am not discounting clinical depression and legitimate disabilities. If you are facing those symptoms, please seek professional help! However, if you are "born" a abuser or alcoholic is there any hope for change or are you justified in staying stuck in a cycle of addiction and waste? That example may seem a bit extreme; however you can keep saying the skunk doesn't stink, but sooner or later someone will call your bluff. Similarly, it took a child to be forthright about the nakedness of the emperor in the *Emperor's New Clothes*. The little girl, observing the procession, was direct in her evaluation of the emperor.

Hans Christian Anderson's tale recounts an emperor who was convinced by two weavers that his new clothes would be invisible to those who were unfit for their positions, stupid or incompetent. Many of his subjects kept up the pretense, as they did not want to appear foolish. However, even after the child yelled out and was joined by others, the emperor did not stop his procession. Why? He was too proud! The emperor's pride caused additional embarrassment not only for himself, but for his followers. He could not face the truth that he was parading through his kingdom stark naked.

Just as the weavers kept adding more and more "invisible clothes" to the emperor, supplementary bad smells will accumulate when piling on new features to existing corrupted code. This will deliver a never ending cycle of corruption, compounding a current problem. It's a good reminder and warning about the importance of who and where you go to solve a problem. The real problems must be addressed from the start if you are to find real solutions.

Code Inspection

Until we completely demoed our two back-to-back bathrooms, we did not know the full extent of the mold and mildew problem. To our horror, we discovered that one of our showers was growing inedible mushrooms weekly. After we found the source of the decay, we then made up specific plans to quickly correct the problem. The work progressed at a brisk pace resulting from reasonable deadlines and a quality team of workers that did not give us imaginary help.

As to mental code, I have known those who have been in counseling for years, with no apparent progress. This situation tells me that the problem is either so huge that additional psychological or physical help is required, or that there really hasn't been honest confrontation and appropriate steps for effective change. Possibly it has become a "comfortable fix" or an excuse to stay the same with no obvious progress or commitment to change. Mold and mildew may be lurking beneath the surface, not discovered until the wall is town down. Just as a child saw through the emperor's pride and inability to see the truth, increased examination will help you see the true picture and any smelly code. It is necessary to confront weaknesses and faults if you are ever to correct the problem. The good news is that you have the power change your code. You don't need to alter who you are, but you will need to use some of the tools and principles you have gathered to refactor some of your existing code. You will also need additional tools to develop new and lasting habits and routines that will reinforce good, healthy code in your muscle memory. (We will discuss more of this topic later.) Many individuals have developed healthy attitudes to overcome extreme difficulty. For example, Sam Burns developed principles that helped him deal with the challenges in his life.

Never Miss a Party

Sam was in a wheelchair as he talked about being brave. He had an enlarged head, a symptom of Progeria, which brings on symptoms of old age. In his 2013 TEDx speech, "Life According to Sam," given when he was just a junior at Foxboro High School in Massachusetts, Sam Burns offered his formula for living a happy life.

With wisdom far beyond his years he shared three principles of advice: not to feel sorry for yourself, surround yourself with positive people and keep moving forward. That's it, although he did add one more thing: never miss a party.

If Sam could have such a positive mental outlook, disabled with little or no possibility of living past his teens, it's possible for you, too, to never miss a party and develop good mental code. Sam beat the odds by living four years longer than most with his condition. He died on January 10, 2014 at seventeen. His TEDx speech has almost thirteen million views at the present time.[3]

Source Files

Source files on a computer contain the actual original code data. It is where I first discovered my website had been hacked. The viral code, which was a worm, appeared on the first line of the source file of every page. Likewise, as you evaluate the source files of your life with your personal magnifier, you may find smelly mental code in the form of attitudes or emotions that are causing a mental fungus that stinks up every page of your life.

After you evaluate your mental code, develop a plan for refactoring. Even if you have a plan in mind now, it will probably take on slight revisions throughout your stages of life. If you presently don't smell skunks or see mushrooms growing from mildew, that doesn't mean they won't in the future decades. It is wise and prudent to gather and clean up your tools as you never know what will show up in your neighborhood. You want to be prepared, especially if you see a slow-moving mound of black and white fur!

 **TOOLS:**

Magnifying Glass to see the source of the problem and distinguish any smelly code in your life; a plan to help you move ahead in your life and projects.

 MINDSETS:

• Examine with magnification different parts of your life to see what areas can be simplified and refactored.

• Identify smelly mental code in the form of attitudes or emotions that are causing a mental fungus that can stink up your life.

• Be aware of self help programs that give a false sense of security with imaginary help. Check them out carefully.

• Compare Sam Burn's mindset with yours. How are you feeling sorry for yourself? Are you surrounding yourself with positive people? Are you moving forward in life with solid goals? What party have you attended lately?

• View the most difficult answer above with magnification, then craft a workable plan for positive change.

115

CHAPTER 20

SUCCESS TOOL: MEASURE your PROGRESS

If you don't have a yardstick to evaluate your success you will probably never live up to your imagined expectations.

How do you measure success? In the music industry, it used to mean getting that illusive record deal, going on tour and having your picture in major magazines. Today, anyone who has been in the entertainment business for any length of time knows that measuring success by those landmarks is not a true yardstick. Most albums never reach platinum status, touring for the most part is grueling for non-stars and stars alike, and with the number of current blogs and online magazines, most anyone can plaster her picture and message across the Internet and fleetingly "feel" famous.

Consider the Beatles, who were rejected by every major record label in the U.K. but got their first break after recording "Love Me Do," their first hit.[1] Even though some would not call working in clubs true success, the Beatles were already successful, playing in clubs for three years as working musicians before launched in the U.S. by Ed Sullivan. They just became more successful as time went on with hit songs, media exposure and a growing fan base. If you don't have a yardstick or measuring tape to evaluate your success you will probably never live up to your imagined expectations.

Yardstick of Success

Though you may not be a musician or an artist, you still have a certain mental yardstick in order to measure success. What is yours? Dawn Steel, a college dropout and a woman with no money or connections, had enough guts and ambition to become president of Columbia Pictures in 1987, the first woman to run a major motion picture studio.

Dawn says about her career, "It's not just luck. It takes work, will, repetition, risk, sometimes making a fool out of yourself, sometimes taking a huge leap of faith. But always remember—it's never too late."[2] She also emphasizes how important it was to take every job seriously and do it better than everyone else. Hers was an attitude of excellence, reflecting good mental code.

Rebound After Striking Out

It's easy to beat yourself up over so-called "failures." Michael Eisner, former CEO of the Walt Disney Company (1984 to 2005), said, "I learned that you have to feel free to fail, that you have to pitch every idea you've got and it doesn't matter if they're bad. Never forget that Babe Ruth wasn't only the home run champ, he was also the strike out champ! No risk, no gain."[3] (Babe Ruth struck out 1,330 times, compared to 714 homeruns.)

To build a muscle is to break it down. With repetition that tires the muscle out, oxygen and blood are sent to the exhausted area, or failed muscle tissue, and the muscle then has what it needs to get stronger. Life is like that. How many times have you struck out or failed? One of the ways to measure good physical fitness is to see how fast your elevated heart rates returns to normal. How fast are you able to rebound after striking out?

You can easily get into the cycle of being bitter and angry about not being where you'd like to be. Actually, using some of that irritation, channeled with constructive steps and goals, will help you change and move forward. However, you have to decide not to stay angry and resentful, as those attitudes and emotions will not only distort future decisions, but also lead to harmful and misleading choices. Realize that when a door of opportunity closes, there's probably a window ajar. If the window's closed, look for the basement. Every house has to have an entrance somewhere, even if it's just a crack in the wall.

> *If the window's closed, look for the basement. Every house has to*
> *have an entrance somewhere, even if it's just a crack in the wall.*

Success Quotient

Are you afraid of success? That may seem like a strange question, but moving up the ladder in any field holds increased responsibility, increased pressure and additional expectations. Some of those expectations may be the added responsibility of public speaking, which is defined as one of the all-time highs of people's fears, also known as *glossophobia*.

It is estimated that as much as seventy-five percent of the population struggles with fear of public speaking to a certain degree--that's 238 million people![4]   What if you find yourself in front of a group and can't remember what you're going to say, even your name? To combat that fear, since 1924, *Toastmasters*[5] has helped over a million people gain the confidence to communicate in any situation. This organization goes to show there's help out there, even for speaking!

What are you using to measure success? Money? Free time? Passion for work? Large audiences? Numbers of products produced? Size of house? Extra recreational toys? Part of your success quotient will be based on your life mission statement, and if you don't have one, you should think seriously about creating even a simple mission statement as it will help you constructively measure success with the good mental code of a defined goal.

> *A mission statement will help you constructively measure success with*
> *the good mental code of a defined goal.*

Your Mission Statement

Most have heard the term "mission statement" as it refers to business. Many mission statements are revealed in advertising slogans. McDonalds' is "To be our customers' favorite place and way to eat and drink." Starbucks is "To inspire and nurture the human spirit— one person, one cup and one neighborhood at a time." Whether or not the mission statement rings true is up to you to decide, and you usually decide by purchasing that specialty drink or product.

Wal-Mart's advertising slogan is in line with their mission statement: "We save people money so they can live better." Costco's mission is to "Continually provide members with quality goods and service at the lowest possible prices." Nordstrom, the high-end department store, labels their mission statement as a "goal." At Nordstrom, their goal is to "provide outstanding service every day, one customer at a time." If you have shopped at Nordstrom's, you realize service is truly what they strive to offer every time you walk in.

If you have not defined what success means in your life,
you will never feel like you've achieved it.

A mission statement will bring clarity to your life and will give you a lucid awareness of your personal achievements as it is measurable. You probably know someone who will never really feel successful, even with money, talent and friends. That person could very well be you. If you have not defined what success means in your life, you will never feel like you've achieved it.

The Thesis of Your Life

When I finished my graduate work, I wrote a thesis, which is an essay involving personal research on a certain premise. This was before the days of Internet and online resources. I spent many hours in the library archives to complete my research. In the same way, though much shorter, your personal mission statement will take some work and is the thesis of your life. It will help you to define and be content with your success. Notice that the corporate mission statements in the section above don't measure success with how many hamburgers, beverages, shopping items or pieces of clothing actually sold. Success is first based upon philosophy and purpose. After a mission statement is declared, long or short term goals can be set and measured more effectively. Your branding statement, which is what you are in the workplace, will also be in line with your mission statement and many times they are similar.

My professional mission statement has changed slightly through the years as I've reinvented myself several times, but the core has stayed the same. I aim to "make a positive impact worldwide, helping others reach their goals in life with books, music, speaking, education, performance and media."

Your personal mission statement is the thesis of your life. It will help you to define your success with a measurable outcome.

If a mission statement is in line with who you are personally and professionally, it will be a tool in obtaining and keeping a positive attitude about your work-life, a balance of good mental code with realistic objectives. If you have already thought through this subject, keep reminders of your mission statement at the forefront of your mind and thoughts. Creating good, healthy, manageable goals with good code will then be obtainable. Remember, your brain is more powerful than any computer and is able to adjust to changes in command. Just as the rudder of a ship keeps it on course, your mission statement will keep you on track with good and positive mental code.

Just as the rudder of a ship keeps it on course, your mission statement will keep you on track with good and positive mental code.

 **TOOLS:**

Yardstick or measuring tape to measure success according to your mission statement; long and short term goals and your branding statements come out of your mission statement.

 MINDSETS:

• Define your personal yardstick of success. If it's subliminal, work on a way to easily define your objectives clearly.

• Note an area you've experienced recent so-called failure in an area of focus. If you have not rebounded after that episode, rebuild your muscle with a plan to create resilience.

• Don't depend on other people's approval for personal success. It is not only dangerous but also extremely discouraging.

• Create your personal mission statement. It is the thesis of your life. It will help you to define your success with a measurable outcome as you are able to then define short and long term goals and your branding statements more successfully.

Ye Old Toolbox

CHAPTER 21

RELATIONSHIP TOOL:
REFINE your FRIENDSHIPS

Good relationships give life and energy to your aspirations;
toxic relationships kill your dreams.

A power belt sander is an easy way to shape and smooth surfaces. The coarser the sandpaper grit, the easier it is to leave deep scratches, difficult to remove. Sandpaper with a lighter grit acts as a smoothing tool to bring out the beauty of a rough surface. Relationships are like diverse grades of sandpaper, either scraping with harshness or inspiring with smoothness.

Ending a relationship that rubs like rough sandpaper is a strenuous challenge for individuals who have difficulty with confrontation or communication. Even though it's difficult to define and eliminate relationships that are gritty, harsh or poisonous, it's necessary, as the deep scratches and toxins can spread like a virus.

Defining your relationships will give you a good start in setting the boundaries for your connections. If you need personal validation from friends and others, you will have a tendency to say "yes" to everyone. Thus, your relationships will have blurred edges with no end in sight.

Relationships are like diverse grades of sandpaper, either
scraping with harshness or inspiring with smoothness.

Spreading Venom

Cheers, an American sitcom that ran for eleven seasons between 1982 and 1993,[1] is a show about rough and smooth relationships. The show, set in a bar named Cheers in Boston, Massachusetts, hosts a group of locals who meet to drink, relax and socialize. The phrase "Where everyone knows your name," was the main hook of the theme song lyric, suggesting that kinship and community served as the bar's main attraction. *Cheers* became a "home away from home" for many. Not all the characters were emotionally healthy, which provided material for good comedy, their backstories ranged from struggles with alcoholism to bigamy. *Cheers* revealed how important human relationships and friendships are, either polishing with encouragement or grating with grittiness, just like different grades of sandpaper.

Another example is the sitcom *Friends,* an American series running for ten seasons (1994 and 2004).[2] The episodes depict the six main characters' comedic, romantic and career issues, all revolving around close friendships. Massive mayhem, family trouble, past and future romances, fights, laughs, tears and surprises were experienced as the characters learned what it really meant to be a "friend." T.V. sitcoms like *Cheers* and *Friends* demonstrate how certain friendships become toxic, spreading venom to poison even healthy circumstances.

There is much talk today about detoxification, the process of removing impurities from the blood in the liver, where toxins are processed for elimination. There are numerous websites and blogs that speak of cleansing diets for your body, but what about for your relationships? How do you detoxify an unhealthy association with a friend or colleague? Defining and replacing what is impure is the first step.

> *Certain friendships become toxic, spreading venom*
> *to poison even healthy circumstances.*

Symptoms of Toxicity

Some of the physical symptoms of toxicity are the same as the emotional symptoms in personal and professional relationships, including fatigue, sluggish elimination, irritated skin, allergies, infections, puffy eyes, bloating and mental confusion. Those physical symptoms result from what is put in the body. In the same way, absorbing the poison of bad and destructive relationships bring on the emotional symptoms of toxicity.

A healthy body can rid itself of toxins more easily than one that is sick. In detoxifying the body, the first step is to drink plenty of liquids, mainly water. Water brings life. The early settlers in our country first looked for water before they would settle on a piece of land, as it was absolutely necessary for survival.

Upon reading a good book, you may feel as though you are drinking in fresh and invigorating water with new thoughts and inspiring messages. A good friend or colleague who encourages you to be your best will make you feel the same way. The relationship will propel you forward with energy, power and new ideas. The opposite is true with an energy-zapping friend or colleague who sucks the life out of you, like a poisonous snake bite. If you have relationships dragging you down, similar to polluted water attacking your digestion, look closely at the social stream where you're swimming.

Polluted Water

When swirling around in muddy water, no amount of clean water will make the water totally clean. In the same way, take a hard, discerning look at those in your close circle of contacts and do a quick personal evaluation of whether they are muddying the clarity of your life. The answer will influence where and with whom you spend the majority of your time. It is absolutely essential, though never easy, to empty a container of bad or unhealthy relationships because water will remain polluted without the ability to purify itself. Likewise, a bad friendship rarely improves on its own.

With water, you can boil it and add bleach to purify it. Unfortunately, you can't boil and bleach relationships and friends to make them pure. However, you can choose not to drink the water or continue certain close friendships and relationships, as one drop of contamination will influence the whole glass and consequently, your whole life.

There is a difference between offering encouragement to those people stuck in a hole, who need a hand up and those living in a hole who pull you down with them. If you find yourself sinking into a cavern of negativity, evaluate your own level of neediness. Why do you pursue friendships that bring negative consequences?

It pays to test the waters of friendship. Dip that toe in the water and make sure it's pure and good. In some relationships, it's difficult to define what's wrong at first. There are,however, people who can suck the air right out of the room. Discovering their motives is at times puzzling. Just as good relationships are compared to clean water, the same principle holds true with the life giving air you breathe.

Fresh Air of Relationships

Taking good deep breaths is very important in physical exercise as well as singing and playing most wind and brass instruments. Expending breath releases toxins and relaxes the body. Breath gives life, even as it did all the way back in the biblical story of creation with Adam and Eve.

Some relationships are beyond recovering and no amount of CPR will resuscitate them. Toxic people who drain you probably won't change. Take, for instance, Andrea Sachs, played by Anne Hathaway in *The Devil Wears Prada*.[3] She is hired as the second assistant to the powerful, sophisticated Miranda Priestly, played by Meryl Streep, a ruthless, merciless fashion magazine editor. As Andrea works hard to deal with Miranda's endless demands, she loses sight of her own life, her loves, and her friends. In the movie, she has to decide what matters most.

Some relationships are beyond recovering and no amount
of CPR will resuscitate them.

Andrea chose to use good mental code and not let the evil Miranda Priestly extract the life and air from her. She found her own voice, and even though she made some personal changes throughout the movie, she preserved her own identity in the process. You can do the same. Exiting a bad situation is not easy, but sometimes it is absolutely essential.

Exiting the Situation

On a recent trip to Costco, I ran into a person I thought I'd never see again. Even though it was an encounter with a former professional acqaintance, it was similar to running into an old friend from high school. Seeing that individual again made me realize how far I had come since I knew him.

Ten years before, several difficult incidents determined the parting of our working relationship. Our goals had become different, but this person was my coach, so it was very difficult to break off our connection. Certain coaches become very possessive and this one was no exception. The issue of control became part of the problem. If I stayed with this same coach, it would mean walking in a circle, just as cattle do, not going anywhere new. I chose instead to take a sharp turn and squeeze down the snaked chute toward an entirely different direction. It was definitely not emotionally easy to do, but exiting the situation proved to be the right decision.

In Costco, I was extremely courteous to my "old friend," but found it fascinating that I felt no emotion or weirdness. I actually felt a bit sorry for this person who seemed unchanged, as I had moved on, learning and expanding in my career. I was in a totally different place emotionally and professionally than I had been ten years before because I had made the mental choice and taken the action to alter my course toward forward growth.

Resolute Courage

Memories came flooding back as I remembered how difficult it was to make the necessary change, especially countering a strong personality. I was reminded of the Theodore Roosevelt statement, "It is only through labor and painful effort, by grim energy and resolute courage that we move on to better things."[4] I realized from that brief encounter that I had absolutely made the correct decision as I now had solid goals, knew my strengths and understood the pace in which I worked. In fact, the rough occurence from years ago made me stronger and more polished today.

There are many different grades, or grits, of sandpaper. Compared to relationships, the rougher the sandpaper, the tougher and more noxious the relationship. A smooth sandpaper is likened to the refining process that happens with healthy relationships. Healthy communication may include conflict and disagreement but is constructive and fosters growth for both sides with refinement and self improvement. As demonstrated with my coach, some relationships can also evolve from smooth to rough with the danger of creating deep grooves without change.

There are many who struggle with making a change as I did. They will continue rotating around a safe place, pointed where those have gone before them. Understanding the power of the snaked chute and breaking that pattern will not only change your mental code, but your life. In the same way, drinking good water and breathing the fresh air of relationships will keep you on track in developing good code.

There are some who take this to an extreme, living in isolation and inaccessibility. Evaluating your own emotional health and neediness helps to return you to a healthy balance. When my dear mother was living through chemotherapy treatments for her stage four breast cancer, her body ached so much that she could hardly hug. In the same way, if you're hurting so much emotionally where you can't touch others, see what type of chemotherapy treatment is poisoning your attitude and life.

In conclusion, understand the "why" of your relationships. If they are to mainly validate your worth, this is a dangerous position as the sandpaper will continue to be too gritty, creating incessant scars, or if too smooth will offer very little benefit to your life. Be free to create different levels of relationships and contacts that are healthy. It will be similar to smiling with sincere warmth when someone asks you out, while you gently refuse, communicating, ever so sweetly, that you are dating someone else. In doing so, you will have just set a realistic boundary. You have also defined your friendship with a healthy attitude and manner.

 ## TOOLS:

Sanding block and sandpaper of friends and relationships rubbing against your life either as rough and toxic or smooth and constructive.

 ## MINDSETS:

• Surround yourself with the types of contacts and close comrades who will encourage, inspire and help you reach your goals. Mom was right: your friends and relationships will define who you are.

• Evaluate any symptoms of fatigue, sluggish elimination, irritated skin, allergies, infections, puffy eyes, bloating and mental confusion. They are are all symptoms of physical and emotional toxicity.

• After identification, empty your glass and life of toxic or unhealthy relationships. Doing so is never emotionally easy and seldom fun, but you can move on to better things with resolute courage and a new cast of characters that help you refine your life with a smooth and constructive rubbing of sandpaper.

• If you find yourself sinking into a cavern of negativity, evaluate your own level of neediness from those in your close circle of contacts.

CHAPTER 22

SPIRITUALITY TOOL: ENERGY and POWER

Without reading the fine print in life, you may find yourself in a Faustian bargain, carried off to an unknown netherworld.

A battery provides power. In your car, the stored chemical energy in the car battery provides electrical energy to start your vehicle and stabilizes the voltage to keep your engine running. In the same way, your spiritual beliefs will either steadily energize you or leave you stranded with no power and regret.

In the 2016 movie *Burnt*,[1] chef Adam Jones (Bradley Cooper), lived with regret. He sentenced himself to shucking one million oysters at a bar in New Orleans for messing up his life with drug use fueled by a manic drive for perfection. His personal penance was voluntary self-punishment for having done wrong. Adam kept track of his oyster-shucking activity in a small pocket notebook, secured with a rubber band.

The purpose of paying penance, which means "be sorry," is not only repentance, but also clearing personal guilt from a particular action. Unfortunately, the penance Adam played out shucking all those oysters didn't help him handle failure, as penance alone didn't solve his root problems. Many find themselves, just like Adam, attempting reparation to obtain a clear conscience and forgiveness when they also need help finding their purpose. They require the power of a spiritual battery to jumpstart their lives.

Larger Than Yourself

Just as shucking oysters didn't solve the root problem for Adam, penance alone won't solve the issue of bad mental code. However, belief in a higher power is a step in the right direction. Trust in a supreme being is absolutely vital in dealing with guilt, shame, failure and the other feelings leading to negative self-talk. Not everyone shares this view; however, many have no idea what they believe in. Thus, they continually search for meaning, wandering in a circle like cattle in a pen.

Speaking of cattle, one of the exercises I do in my early-morning workouts at the gym is called Dairyman. It is not one of my favorite exercises; although I'm not sure I have any favorite exercises! Imagine the old-time dairyman carrying a sloshing bucket of milk in each hand. He has to keep good balance and pace so as not to spill the milk. The Dairyman exercise is similar to carrying those two buckets except that heavy weights, not milk, are involved.

Carrying the Weight

On several occasions, I have been approached at the gym by well-mannered gentlemen who offer to carry my two thirty-five pound weights. Even though it's tempting to take them up on their offer, I always smile and insist it's a part of my workout. I know the only way I can become stronger is to carry those weights, which are heavy, but not too heavy, for my body frame.

Becoming stronger in life results from a similar action. Belief in God doesn't provide you with a magic lamp with multiple wishes to take away problems, such as sickness, death, or tragedy. However, a belief in a supreme being as a source of power does allow you to share the load, not carrying more weight than you can handle.

Belief in a supreme being as a source of power does provide you with the ability to share the load, not carrying more weight than you can handle.

Genie or Judge?

Everyone has some spiritual belief, whether it is belief in no God, in an angry God, a judging God, a God manifest in objects, or a God who cares and watches over you. Thoughts of God and the hereafter approach swiftly, with intensifying succession in times of tragedy, failure, danger, or illness.

Guilt is a genuine emotion. At times, guilt feelings can provide the motivation for positive change and desire for repentance, yet most of the time, unresolved guilt is destructive. Guilt breaks down healthy confidence, instigates hopelessness, brings depression, and even makes a talented chef shuck a million oysters, as in the movie *Burnt*.

The power to change comes with the belief that there is something bigger than yourself that will give you the strength to break free.

Living under the heavy blanket of guilt brings the bad mental code of a continual sequence of blame, never getting out from under that weighty blanket of self-criticism. The power to change comes with the belief that there is something bigger than yourself that will give you the strength to break free, as stated in the *Power of Peace Project*.

Breaking Free

I met Kit Cummings at a cable T.V. taping when he was just starting his *Power of Peace Project* shortly after 2010. Kit is an engaging speaker with an impactful message. The *Power of Peace Project* began when Kit started bringing the message of peace, hope and change into the most difficult places in America—prisons.

On January 18, 2011, twelve men at a dangerous maximum security prison signed the "Power of Peace Pledge" along with the accompanying principles and challenges. They set out to see if the men in Georgia's toughest prison could work with the principles of the "Power of Peace Pledge." Unknowingly, those bold men, some whom were former gang members, serving life sentences, started a national Peace Movement that would spread to many other state prisons and schools across America.[2]

One of the books Kit wrote is *40 Days of Prayer* to link the wounded communities between schools, prisons and churches. With solid, proven principles, accompanied with prayer, Kit successfully energized a very successful movement.

Men began to practice a lifestyle of non-violence and word spread. Instead of being labeled as "weak," those men gained a new kind of respect among the prison population. Commitment to those principles also helped participants in breaking free from the destructive bad code of anger, violence and hate. The Power of Peace Pledge has produced a contract with far-reaching benefits, contrasted with agreements that are misleading or even deceptive.

Read the Fine Print

When 75,000 shoppers unknowingly sold their souls as part of an April Fools Day gag for a popular computer game, it was because 88 percent of the people who bought the game didn't read the fine print in the terms and conditions clause.[3] How often do you read the terms and conditions of any contract for a downloadable computer program? If you're like most, not often! You simply press the "agree" button to quickly move on.

The condition of your soul is more valuable than fine print in a contract. It is at the central core of your being. You may remember the classic German legend of *Faust*, the highly successful scholar who sold his soul to the Devil, in exchange for knowledge and worldly pleasures. However, it didn't work out particularly well for him. In the end, the Devil triumphantly carries him off to Hell. Without reading the fine print in life, you also may find yourself in a Faustian bargain, carried off to an unknown netherworld.

The condition of your soul is more valuable than fine print in a contract.
It is at the central core of your being.

Don't Sell Your Soul

This is not a book to convince or convert you spiritually, but unless you read the fine print and face the condition of your spiritual life and soul in the same way as other areas of your life, the same questions of purpose, doubt and guilt will keep recurring as negative self-talk. Many are in the cycle of paying penance over and over. In fact, Adam Jones in *Burnt* wasn't free from his burden of self-punishment and guilt, even after throwing his small notebook into the ocean. Jones needed more than penance or belief in a spikey red living thing to guide him on his road to recovery. He needed to take action with a reliable source of battery power that could free him from his mental demons of bad code. A reliable battery is one that is not corroded, sitting on the shelf. Some believe they have a spiritual battery with a past belief or decision, but have left it sitting on the shelf for so long that it is powerless to do the job it was meant for.

I believe in a supreme God and creator and am at peace with that decision. There are many things I don't understand, but I don't always understand certain math and physics principles either. Knowing and believing in my maker and a God who is personal in my life gives me the individual freedom not to feel guilt or pay penance with shame for every feeling of remorse that occurs.

Paying attention to the condition of your soul is a part of developing and maintaining good mental code.

It takes just as much faith not to believe in any sort of Supreme being or higher power as to believe in an ultimate creator. Paying attention to the condition of your soul is a part of developing and maintaining good mental code. That belief will recharge you emotionally and mentally, just as a battery does.

 **TOOLS:**

A battery of spiritual belief that is the power and strength behind your emotional thoughts and mental code.

 MINDSETS:

• Determine what source of higher power you depend on. Penance alone won't solve the issue of bad mental code of shame and guilt. With a true power source, you will gain the strength and purpose to break free from the cycle of the negative mental code of unworthiness.

• Define an area where you are carrying emotional weight that is sometimes heavy. It can end up making you more resilient and sturdy with solid balance and control.

• Don't sell your soul and be the victim of a Faustian bargain. The condition of your soul is more valuable than fine print in a contract. It is at the very central core of your being.

• Pay attention to the condition of your soul. It is a part of developing and maintaining good mental code. That belief will recharge you emotionally, just as a battery does. Everyone has some sort of spiritual belief, whether it is belief in no God, in an angry God, a judging God, a God manifest in objects, or a God who cares and watches over you.

• If you have a spiritual battery with a past belief or decision but have left it sitting on the shelf for so long that it is powerless to do the job it was meant to do, clean the terminals and renew your commitment to regain its power in your life.

CHAPTER 23

AUTHENTIC TOOL:
IDENTIFY and REFLECT

Some are afraid to look in the mirror to view what is truly there.
Honest reflection is a tool for positive change.

Clothing stores are very aware of the value of a good mirror. In fact, different curves in a mirror, slightly outward or inward, can make you look heavier or thinner and influence sales. However, a true reflection is vital in determining your genuine and authentic image. This is illustrated simply, yet effectively in this literary fairy tale.

The little duckling wandered away from his barnyard home after being teased about his homeliness. When he sees a flock of migrating wild swans, he tries to follow them, but he is too small, can't fly and almost freezes to death.

The young duck is rescued by a farmer who takes him to his farmhouse. However, he is frightened and runs away again because he does not fit in with the other farm animals. When spring arrives, the flock of wild swans returns, flying gracefully to the lake where they swim proudly. The little duckling, awed by their performance, moves closer. At the water's edge, the young bird notices his beautiful, expansive wings and takes flight with his new family. Finally, he sees his true reflection that reveals who he really is--not a duckling at all, but a graceful swan. Just as the young cygnet found, a mirror or pool of reflection acts as an important tool in determining who you really are.

Want to be a Horse?

The Ugly Duckling is an often-told treasured story, especially for young children. However, the message remains relevant as you are often faced with glossy ads that tell you how beautiful, slim or muscular you need to look. Those images don't reflect what most people face when they wake up and look at their reflection in the mirror. In fact, the number of disparaging features grows larger as you age.

Today, *The Ugly Duckling* may be told like this: A little duckling sees a flock of migrating wild swans but can't follow them because he can't fly. However, the farmer pampers to assuage his pain, giving him a farm participant ribbon, and tells him he can be anything he wants through his imagination. So the little duckling decided he wants to be a horse as he'd be able to run through the meadow and jump over fences, swiftly and freely.

Your Reflection

So he practices and practices until he is able to waddle from one end of the farm to the other. He also rehearses his "neigh" but only expends ugly snort, honk, click and hissing sounds. The harder he envisions his future and the longer he practiced, the more discouraged he becomes. One day, while looking at his reflection, he is horrified he is growing wings instead of legs and hooves. He finds them ugly and not becoming for a creature that would gallop through the forest. He momentarily ponders cutting them off. In addition, his complexion is growing paler each day. Sadly, the ugly duckling didn't realize that his wings would allow flight and his coloring would change as he grew the beautiful white, soft feathers of a magnificent swan.

What do you see in your reflection? Are you seeing a want-to-be horse, an idolized model, or do you see your potential, your uniqueness, your beauty and talents? Many times we compare ourselves to others or to a fantasy of what we think we want to be, but we fail to see who we really are. The duckling, when pampered, was sheltered from the reality that he would go through a period of development when his appearance would change. Because he did not look like everyone else, he became so disgusted with his own wings, so much so that he wanted to hurt himself. Since feelings of inadequacy and low-self esteem are rampant especially among youth, realistic expectations, quality communication and acceptance are more important than ever.

Many times we compare ourselves to what we think we want to be, but fail to see what we really are.

I've Gotta Be Me

"What else can I be but what I am," are lyrics from the song, "I've Gotta Be Me," a popular song from the 1968 Broadway musical *Golden Rainbow*. Even though the musical wasn't a great success, when Sammy Davis Jr. recorded the song, it became a surprise hit.

Another line in the song says "I can't be right for somebody else if I'm not right for me." The song focuses on success and working hard for a dream or prize. Those lyrics are contrasted with the message of the recent book *Generation Me*.[1] Dr. Jean Twenge, PhD, uses data from over eleven million respondents born in the 1980s and 1990s, defining them as tolerant, confident, open-minded and ambitious, but also disengaged, narcissistic, distrustful and anxious: "Recent high school graduates are more likely to want lots of money and nice things, but less likely to say they're willing to work hard to earn them."[2]

Espinoza and Ukleja in *Managing the Millennials,* said, "Due to technology, Millennials are the first generation that does not need an authority figure to access information."[3] Without reliable guidance, self-absorption leads to doubt and frustration. "Participant" trophies are awarded, as many are afraid a loss will damage their precious darling's desire to compete. However, without obstacles and hurdles, we develop a generation that expects results without the sweat and work it takes to get there. There is a balance to be found in healthy self-acceptance and self-improvement.

There is nothing wrong with working hard to improve yourself, however when observing *Muscle and Fitness*[4] magazine's cover photo of a model with sculpted abs, pumped biceps and a small waist, the image can be disconcerting. The magazine advertises that with certain exercises you, too, can get a ripped body. These photos are often manipulated by a computer and do not accurately represent the actual physique of the model but is an unrealistic representation. Plus, who can tell what additional supplements and other enhancing compounds are being used by the model? So why compare? (If you're like most, you can't help it!)

The Magic Mirror

I have a small mirror I use when teaching voice that I call the "magic mirror." The mirror itself is only a couple inches high, but it does wonders in observing, then correcting, the jaw when singing. After using the mirror for even a very short time, viewers are able to make simple changes to relax the jaw with very little effort. The mirror encourages the correct position by giving voice students positive reinforcement and immediate recognition.

Looking in a mirror also reveals blemishes and tight clothes. Some days, it's emotionally easier to ignore the mirror, but knowledge and truth is power. Your true reflection will give you transforming power. Some are afraid to look in the mirror to view their honest reflection, ignoring its ability to encourage positive change.

In the same way, video is also a great tool. However, without some confidence, watching yourself will be damning rather than constructive. With all the silly short videos out now on YouTube and other channels, it should be easier to be less self-critical, but for many, it's not easy to see themselves on camera. "Too fat," "too old," "bad hair day," bad face day," are the many comments and outward observations that people make about their video images.

Without some confidence, watching yourself
will be damning rather than constructive.

How do you combat the fear, the anxiety, the self-doubt and lack of confidence that paralyzes and constricts opportunity and growth with negative mental code? Are the lyrics, "I've gotta be me" even relevant today? Most know that what's seen on the outside doesn't always reflect what's on the inside, but what's on the outside can be so disheartening that what's on the inside can't or won't be revealed.

Your Authentic Self

Showing some of my videos to a speaking coach was risky—I am definitely guilty of focusing on my appearance, what I wear, my hair, weight and rate of speaking, with an intense over-analysis that I struggle to overcome. However, this particular coach saw in less than a minute the authenticity and sincerity in my presentation. That was good news to me as a healthy view of self is not boastful and arrogant, but confident and assured. It means much more than the confidence portrayed on a glossy magazine cover.

What's on the outside can be so disheartening that what's on
the inside can't or won't be revealed.

I was so focused on how I looked that I didn't see what the coach saw. When I started producing more videos, I recalled the coach's observation and realized how her one comment freed me to be myself. While my hair and overall look are still important, authenticity and sincerity are valuable traits when I portray a message focused on helping others. To be genuine and confident are significant attributes. Even with that small bit of feedback, I could delete some bad code of self-doubt in relaying an honest and heartfelt message.

Honesty

Billy Joel, American pianist, singer and songwriter, describes "honesty" as a lonely word, as everyone is so untrue. Joel also sings that honesty is hardly ever heard and mostly what he needs to hear. The lyrics of "Honesty," released in 1979 still ring true, more today than ever.[5]

Honesty from a trusted friend or colleague acts as a true source of reflection to help you see the image of your thoughts, actions and personality. Those relationships may even act as light sandpaper to sharpen you and give you important, needed feedback. They will not fill your ears with flattery that will artificially curve a mirror in or out to persuade you with their personal agenda. Those manipulated images fade just as quickly as a slick magazine cover.

I have groups of honest friends who will give me authentic feedback and encouragement. They help me see my true reflection as I'm able to verbalize my thoughts and dreams. The often quoted phrase, "Iron sharpens iron"[6] was written when iron didn't have the same qualities that it does today. It was not as hard and had many impure qualities that would be sloughed off and sharpened when rubbed against another piece of iron.

Authentic friends will not fill your ears with flattery
that will artificially curve a mirror in or out to
persuade you with their personal agenda.

In the same way, evaluate your own responses and attitudes as you rub up against other personalities. In doing so, you will learn more about yourself, mirroring areas of weakness that need either shedding or improvement. Such personal evaluation takes honesty and a willingness to look at your authentic reflection. You may not run through the meadow and jump over fences, but you can fly with magnificent wings and realize you are beautiful just as you are.

 **TOOLS:**

Mirror to see your authentic reflection; healthy and honest relationships that will give you truthful feedback and help you sharpen your life.

 MINDSETS:

• Identify your true reflection. Actually look in a mirror to see what is really there. Many times we compare ourselves to what think we want to be, but fail to see what we really are.

• Celebrate who you are right now. Find balance in healthy self-acceptance and self-improvement. There is nothing wrong with wanting to improve your looks or your attributes as long as you know who and what you are.

• Look at your positive attributes as well as areas of improvement. Reflection is a tool for positive change if you are not over-critical.

• Realize that attention to the outward appearance is important, but if the heart and the message aren't related in a genuine, honest way, the impact will be minimal. Review your personal mission statement as your life message.

• Don't be afraid to gain valuable feedback from people in your life. As you rub up against other personalities, you will learn more about yourself, discovering areas of weakness that need either shed or improved upon.

PART THREE
DECADES OF CODE

Shifting Forms of Bad Code
Through the Decades

CHAPTER 24

MASTERING CODE THROUGH THE DECADES

For new, healthy code to have lasting results, segments must be reinforced over and over again during thousands of precise repetitions.

Mastery means to gain control. To master code through the decades is to first understand the changes that take place. Consequentially, you will use the tools necessary to modify and operate at maximum effectiveness, especially in incorporating the myelin sheath in developing muscle memory.

As a professional figure skater, Scott Hamilton was a strong believer in muscle memory. He chose to have every step in his short and long program memorized, right down to the number of crossovers before an attempted Lutz or toe loop.[1]

In his memoir, *My Losing Season*, Pat Conroy described his senior season as the starting point guard on the 1966-67 basketball team at The Citadel. He said, "In sports there are no natural athletic gifts that cannot be improved and shaped by the power of discipline."[2] Similarly, you have the power to master your mental code and replace negative mental code with positive mental code through the power of muscle memory using consistent repetition.

Secret Codes

Conroy spent hours of lonely periods of practice to incorporate new moves into his game. He memorized every move by breaking segments down into its components. He then practiced those segments over and over during thousands of precise repetitions. "You move, you react, you recover, you drive, and the thinking is seamless and invisible in the secret codes of your game."[3]

For new, healthy code to have lasting results, segments must be reinforced over and over again during thousands of precise repetitions, just as Pat did in basketball. As a result, when you get in the game, your responses to the basics of the game will be natural and automatic resulting from spending time on those drills.

Myelin Sheath

The myelin sheath (mentioned in earlier chapters) is a powerful method to change code. Myelin, which is a whitish sheath that insulates many nerve fibers connecting neurons (nerve cells) together, helps a person reinforce good habits. The myelin builds as impulses, or neurons move faster and faster with repetition. Those neurons increase in firing speed, according to Dr. Daniel Siegel up to 3,000 times faster when a repetitive action is performed.[4]

This principle can be used positively or negatively in the circumstances of your life. If there is constant danger or abuse, verbal or physical, those continuous mental messages of fear and lack of confidence are difficult to overcome. The average person has 70,000 thoughts per day; this breaks down to about 3,000 per hour, fifty per minute and close to one new thought per second. If you subtract sleep time, it is over one per second.[5] That can be overwhelming unless you break down that fear and reticence with new, consistent, constructive signals to the nerve and brain.

When new signals are created and the myelin sheath is strengthened, you are actually producing new neurons to reshape certain areas of the brain, known as neuroplasticity. The new neurons that are created are known as neurogenesis. You don't have to be a psychologist or psychotherapist to understand the importance of positive repetition on the brain and your habits.

You don't have to be a psychologist or psychotherapist to understand the importance of positive repetition on the brain and your habits.

Talent or Training?

I was born with a certain amount of natural talent, particularly in music. From a young age I was able to hear a melody and create it almost instantly by ear, especially on a piano. I picked up improvisation and writing music quite easily. Early on, I had a teacher who taught me the chords and basics of music while also encouraging me to perform with both piano and voice. I loved it.

Upon entering high school, I changed instructors to begin studying classical music more seriously. I entered the wonderful studio of Joanna Hodges, the first woman concert pianist to tour communist Russia. Joanna was warm, yet strict, always dressing in black and wearing her hair piled on top of her head. She quickly inserted the discipline and rigor into my practice schedule that would pay significant dividends throughout my life and career.

To study in Joanna's studio was to perform and compete, often. For our first competition, I was to play the slow, middle movement of the *Haydn Sonata in Eb*. It was different than most of the flashy arrangements I had previously performed, but I had no doubts in my ability to handle it. I prepared, not as thoroughly as I should, but depended on my performance skills and ear.

When it came time for the competition, I was fairly excited. My mother let me get my hair done at the beauty school, and they piled it on top of my head. I felt fairly special, also wearing my new green dress. After arriving at the competition site, I knew soon it was my turn to compete. Upon entering the room, walking proudly, shoulders back, I handed my music to the three judges and sat on the piano bench.

Once I put my hands on the piano keys, I immediately remembered I was to play the slow middle movement of the *Haydn Sonata in Eb*, but nothing else. My mind was blank. Wait! I remembered part of the melody. No problem! I fell back on all that "natural talent" and soon made up who-knows-what. With a nice ending, I reveled in my accomplishment as I stood up, smiled at the judges while taking my music, (I doubt if they smiled back!) and exited the room.

Joanna greeted me with, "How did you do?" I responded, "Well, parts of the piece just left me. I'm not sure what happened; but no worries. I really did some wonderful things with the melody and I'm sure they were very impressed." She was not smiling.

What it Takes to Win

Fortunately, I wasn't dropped from her studio that day. I had not prepared and mastered the piece correctly since I was depending on the notion of natural talent. If I had been judged from a 1-10, I would have received a "0." That failure proved an important lesson. Preparation is vital for successful performance.

For example, Kobe Bryant spent years getting to the gym very early to practice every move slowly, each hand, each foot separately. He broke down basic drills with repetition so when he got in the game, those moves would be natural. Just like Kobe, I want to win. In fact, after that first competition, I started studying, hard. Soon I was receiving "7's," "8's" and even "10's." I prepared with precise repetition by slowing sections down so when I got in the competition game, the piano moves came naturally, mastered with precise repetition.

I have heard many excuses from those who are approaching midlife as they feel they won't be able to pick up an instrument and play again, or learn a new skill. To that statement, I point out psychologist K.A. Ericsson's research and belief that the drop-off in performance has nothing to do with age, but with shifting priorities. In fact, he found that when older pianists keep up deliberate practice, they perform almost as well as younger ones, even though their fingers are less nimble and brains a little slower.[6]

Mastering a Skill

Many studies say it takes at least 10,000 hours to master a skill, and I put in at least that amount. However, I realize along with those hours of repetition came my lateral natural ability to hear music, play it without written music, along with the capability to focus and integrate those skills. I realized during that fateful first competition that development requires focused practice and repetition, not just natural talent.

*Emotional commitment with accurate, specific
repetition will bring certain change.*

To truly master a skill, you need to own it through deliberate practice, playing through the same section over and over again, accurately. It is usually true that those in their younger years train harder as they don't have as many outside responsibilities. However, most can take on that young mindset of preparation and be extremely successful in owning a skill. This principle also applies to changing a habit or skill. Emotional commitment with accurate, specific repetition will bring certain change.

Cal Newport, in *So Good They Can't Ignore You*, says, "If you can figure out how to integrate deliberate practice into your own life, you have the possibility of blowing past your peers in your value, as you'll likely be alone in your dedication to systematically getting better."[7] Deliberate repetitive action reinforces the myelin sheath, which plays a huge role in your ability to replace and change habits.

Deliberate repetitive action reinforces the myelin sheath, which plays a huge role in your ability to replace and change habits.

Foundation of Preparation

In any game of sports, as in life, there are unexpected balls that are thrown your way, but you can better respond to those zingers if you have a solid foundation of preparation. You can also respond to corrupt accusations of bad mental code, which are discouragement, self-doubt, anxiety and depression. If you have and use good and solid tools to develop positive mental code, you can combat negative self-talk.

Andrew D. Bernstein, a top sports photographer, recently photographed what has become the most-viewed shot of Kobe Bryant's last game on April 13, 2016. He recounts in an interview how important preparation is and that success, like luck, doesn't just happen. You need to plan for it and be prepared for it. Bernstein knew the exact details of not only game logistics, but also options of how Kobe would be exiting the game, placing cameras in three or four different locations and angles to get the one shot he needed.[8] He actually spent many more hours in preparation than in photographing the game.

In the same way, look at your options of preparation after identifying areas of bad code in your own life. Then define your personal plan of deliberate repetition of good positive mental code. Only then can you go about strategizing what will work for your personality and lifestyle. The tools you acquire during any decade of your life will help to sustain you through the changes that life brings. However, you have to use them with repeated practice and repetition to truly master code.

MINDSETS:

• Commit to the required precise repetition needed to reinforce new, healthy code in your life for lasting results.

• Visualize your healthy mental code becoming stronger when new signals are created and the myelin sheath is strengthened. You are actually producing new neurons to reshape certain areas of the brain, known as neuroplasticity.

• Decide to use the mental tools you acquire with repeated practice and repetition to truly master code. An unused tool sitting in your mental toolbox may gleam and glisten, but will prove useless unless used.

• Remove any beliefs that your age hinders you from learning a new skill. It is never too late until you face your own personal final code.

CHAPTER 25

CHANGING CODE
THROUGH THE DECADES

*Throughout every decade lurks dangerous malware of the mind,
waiting to enter your thoughts and brain to
destroy healthy mental code.*

If you've lived any number of years, you realize there are changes that occur every decade of your life. Some of the principles as authenticity, spirituality and relationships stay the same, but methods become slightly different as age and experience merge.

Every generation bears a societal name and characteristic that reflects the times in which they are living. How do you deal with the mental code that aging through the decades brings? At twenty, life seems limitless, even though one is still gaining traction and direction. From then on, it is easy to skid into the following years without the tools to confront a changing mental code through the decades that can bring sabotage and destruction.

It's impossible to put a simple description on a generation, with differing cultures, backgrounds, education and influences. However, life stories are powerful and the validity and authenticity of a personal story with principles of change are hard to deny. Where one person struggles, another succeeds. The following chapters carry some of the personal stories that typify the tools used and needed to achieve success in every decade.

Charmed Life

I was sitting across the table with a professional colleague, sipping my coffee when he suddenly said, "It sounds like you've had a charmed life." Of course, I immediately thought of Disney princesses and fairy-tale magic. After pulling my thoughts together, I responded that yes, it probably sounded that way as I described my amazing family and past. However, in doing so, I pointed out that my life had not been stress free.

Even though I've worked for the Disney Corporation for a number of years and love the fairy tale *Beauty and the Beast*, that doesn't mean I have experienced a charmed life, as even fairy tales record tremendous obstacles faced by the heroine. I have struggled and pushed through my share of unexpected uphill ascents, didactic decisions and career altering requisites. Many of you have done the same.

Some have pushed through great tragedy such as death and cataclysmic destruction, which fortunately I have not had to experience. However, it's not always a disadvantage, but the opposite as it creates resilience and endurance.[1] Whatever your background, it is important to keep learning and growing as your brain continues to change throughout your lifetime.

Your Personal Toolbox

No matter what decade, you need a toolbox. Everyone's toolbox will look as different as variety of hair color, physical types and personalities, but the tools remain similar for each. Start with the tool of eliminating items in your home and life that clutter your thoughts and your work.

Both the offensive and defensive tools you set up will determine how you weather phishing and spear-phishing attacks on your mind.

For those in their twenties and thirties, encumbrances include not only physical aspects but career choices that are not the best. This is applied a little differently in every decade, as children come then leave, job situations change, health challenges occur and downsizing begins. Just as eliminating stuff and non-essential projects is imperative, removing or channeling thoughts of discouragement, apathy and anger to create good mental code takes concentration and focused repetition to generate new habits and goals through each decade. Consequently, understanding the power of the myelin sheath is extremely helpful.

Connecting the Dots

Throughout every decade lurks dangerous malware of the mind, waiting to enter your thoughts and brain to destroy good and healthy mental code. Both the offensive and defensive tools you set up will determine how you weather phishing and spear-phishing attacks on your mind.

You may have fear of the unknown, be stuck in a nightmare where you are crouched low in the front seat of a car, waiting for the inevitable terror attack. If you can't wake yourself up and change your dream, it's time to make some drastic changes in your life or you could find yourself giving up completely.

Both the offensive and defensive tools you set up will determine how you weather phishing and spear-phishing attacks on your mind.

To actively combat the bad mental code that disrupts and damages your life, every generation has to make a conscious intellectual choice. The fact you have faced a certain principle or obstacle one time doesn't mean you'll never face it again; it may appear in a new and different way in an approaching decade. It may look different on the outside, but usually holds a common denominator or principle at its core.

As a pianist, I'm always interested in learning styles and helping others learn, no matter what age. The word "plastic" means molded or pliable. Neuroplasticity, especially related to the myelin sheath is a powerful principle in learning new skills or changing code. Your brain has that ability to mold a new habit.

Importance of Routine

There are no promises of fairy tales as you plod stubbornly through the insanities of life, but you have the ability to develop the tools to establish good mental code. The obstacles are plenty; however, there is a snaked chute of change that provides an alternative from merely circling around the same habit and pattern of your past that may be comfortable, but destructive.

A good, healthy routine is similar to a good rut; it is a management tool. It will free you up from the mundane to focus on the important.

A beneficial routine with focused repetition and precise patterns will help you develop a new skill, no matter what decade of life. When I was studying and practicing for major piano competitions, routine was very important. It allowed me to concentrate and train most effectively to prepare for times of increased pressure.

A good, healthy routine is similar to a good rut; it is a management tool. It will free you up from the mundane to focus on the important. For those in creative fields, a routine to accomplish the ordinary frees up the brain to construct the extraordinary. Applying the patterns of routine will also help you adjust throughout the various decades of your life. Each season has its own fluctuations and challenges and with the capability to add a healthy routine, content may shift, but the management tools will carry you through adjustments and variations.

*A routine to accomplish the ordinary frees up the brain
to construct the extraordinary.*

Development of Routine

Throughout the twenties and thirties, many deal with a sense of entitlement that is sure to bring failure. The importance of building career capital is easily lost within the popularity and focus on merely following your passion. A wealth of knowledge and experience is to be found from listening to and learning from those who have gone before, even though they may talk and move more slowly as the years progress. Developing habits and a good routine will help you glean even more.

With the capability to add a healthy routine, content may shift but management tools will carry you through adjustments and variations.

Looking at the other end of the scale in years, today's world brings virtual communication that happens faster than the speed of sound and light. It is admirable to see those approaching their later decades keep up with some of the technology. However, even as there have been scams and deception in every stage of history, the modern world holds its own unique challenges with hacking, phishing, malware and computer viruses that can destroy entire networks and rob life savings from the vulnerable. Vigilance is vital. Developing habits of consulting a trusted circle of support has never been more important for those facing their later years.

For those in the middle decades, it truly is a challenging time. Living in today's world is uncertain, fostering worry and fear for an indeterminate future. Fortunes can change overnight with an unexpected health crisis or family tragedy. More than ever, there are crushing responsibilities of not only caring for parents and other loved ones, but each younger generation that must still search for their life's work and a way to sustain a living in today's fluxing economic climate. However, it is also an exciting time with more opportunity than ever to reinvent your life and work for many more years due to medical advances that enable many to outlive their predecessors with increased quality of life. Developing the routine and attitude of a lifelong learner is a valuable asset that will continue to encourage good code and healthy mental self-talk.

Development as a Lifelong Learner

At any stage, if you wear the attitude of a lifelong learner with a beginner's mindset, that approach will carry you through most challenges with good positive self-talk. Solid goals with even very small and consistent baby steps will keep you focused and on track, into your eighties and beyond.

Developing a routine that is flexible to change during the decades is healthy and important for creating successful patterns of achievement, good health, fitness, and even relaxation. Add to your recipe of success a support group with just a few trusted friends, or even a roomful of people who will encourage you in your life's journey. It takes vigilance to evaluate and garner the support that is helpful, and eliminate what is obstructive to your objectives. Develop the tenacity and resolve to create and maintain good mental code through the fluctuations life brings.

> *It takes vigilance to evaluate and garner the support that is helpful, and eliminate what is obstructive to your objectives.*

Truly, everyone has a story. It doesn't cost much to lend a listening ear, only a little time. As I started interviewing individuals for this book, I was reminded time and time again how much people love to tell their story. It's hard to capture the tapestry of a life in words on a page, then consider and choose several paragraphs for a book that will relay an impactful message. I found stories of perseverance through stage four cancer, of failed entitlement yet success in learning about life, of misguided information yet also of renewed hope. There are stories of health wake-up calls, of courage and of perseverance through incredible odds and of the awareness and power of changing the direction of one's life.

As you explore the discussion of each decade, you will find principles that apply at every stage of life. However, there are certain characteristics that occur during each period. There is no way that you can define the years with absolute labels, but I think you'll find the description of tendencies extremely helpful.

MINDSETS:

• Embrace your personal story. Your story will change and adjust throughout your decades of life. How you respond to those changes depends on your mental code.

• Take note of the specific principles of each decade that will apply to your life. There is no way you can define the decades of life with absolute labels, but there are certain principles that apply to each.

• Start identifying, collecting or adding quality tools to your personal toolbox now.

• Don't "overanalyze," the different stages of your life, but be realistic with a good picture or snapshots of where you are.

• Establish a routine that will work for you. A good routine is your friend. You can still be flexible and fun with an agenda and schedule. In fact, it will give you freedom.

• Choose your group of close friends carefully. Friends and a circle of support are vital through every decade of life.

CHAPTER 26

TRACTION
IN THE TWENTIES

Career paths in the twenties are a time of shifting tectonic plates,
with the many life changes that occur.

Like many, I remember feeling very grown up in my twenties. However, also like many, I was unsure of what I wanted to do with my life, even with a college, or a graduate degree. Today, depending on the degree and emphasis, many college grads find themselves with great student loan debt, flipping burgers or changing jobs every couple years, wondering where they'll ultimately land. Still others are professional students, altering their career course several times, trying to figure out their passion. This brings on discouragement, disillusionment and even depression for countless young graduates as they aim for traction and momentum to get somewhere in life.

Numerous former as well as current students find themselves in the pursuit of their passion yet do not have the career capital to gain enough traction for success. Cal Newport, in *So Good They Can't Ignore You* says of pursuing passion, "You must first build up rare and valuable skills to offer."[1] Many entering todays marketplace are greeted with the sudden reality that a degree by itself doesn't guarantee a good job or even a job in their field of emphasis.

Grasping for Control

At times I've been inclined, with persuasion, to try something outside my comfort zone. Biking down from the Mammoth Mountain Gondola was one of those occasions. My husband and I were mountain biking and were on our way up to the top, quickly ascending to 11,053 feet. As one not fond of heights, I tentatively looked down. I was wondering how I would manage the small winding path leading us to the bottom.

Many entering today's marketplace are greeted with the sudden reality
that a degree by itself doesn't guarantee a good job
or even a job in their field of emphasis.

As I contemplated my dilemma, an additional visual entered into my consciousness. There were those running up the hill, sliding on the gravel as they grasped for control on the steep climb. It served as a good illustration of the reality of the twenties: trying to gain traction on loose gravel, running uphill.

With footings that are off-balance, encompassing self-esteem to entitlement; it takes tremendous grit to maneuver the uneven surfaces of the decade of the twenties. Much of education exposes you to a variety of possibilities and fields. It's easy to feel pressured to decide exactly what you want to do, even after several years of study. However, it's very healthy to keep an open mind while building the type of skills that contribute to career capital.

The reality of the twenties: trying to gain traction
on loose gravel, running uphill.

Show Me the Way

Pat O'Donnell, at twenty-seven, was desperate about finding what to do with his life. His father urged him to go into engineering so he complied, but hated it. His passion was rock climbing. Through a number of events, using the management tool of weighing his options and the success tool of defining what he really wanted, he landed in Aspen in 1993. Pat became CEO of Aspen Skiing Company in 1996, retiring in 2006.[2]

When asked how he arrived at a resort in Aspen, Pat responded that upon first moving to Yosemite Valley, after quitting his lucrative job as an engineer, he took a job as a bellman at ninety cents an hour. It included a tent, all he could eat free meals and the freedom to climb six hours a day, so that was his entrance into the hospitality business. I wonder what his father thought of this career move!

It's hard to establish what life values you really want in your twenties. Even though Pat didn't ultimately stay the course in engineering, he did finish his education, adding to his bank of career assets creating a well-rounded understanding of design and structure. When seeking his new position, he examined the script of his life, then fulfilled his passion, not wanting to be on his deathbed questioning, "What if?" Apparently, Pat made the right choice in his twenties as he was inducted in the Ski and Snowboard Hall of Fame in 2007, in his sixties.

Mud Run

Aaron Copas chose to join the Marines right out of high school. As well as a tent and all he can eat, he also got a paid trip to Afghanistan and Iraq, at times on the front lines. Aaron is a friend of one of our sons and has shared dinner with us on our patio several times. However, I got to know him further at a mud run at Camp Pendleton outside beautiful San Diego, California. I knew Aaron had been in the Marines, but I was not sure what he did and why he chose to enlist.

I was an observer that day while Aaron, his girlfriend, my son and husband completed the 10K mud run. After taking a number of pictures and hosing off mounds of caked-on dirt, we walked by some of the huge machinery on the expansive base. Aaron remarked how he had worked on many vehicles that were very similar during his enlistment overseas. At that point, I didn't know Aaron was just twenty-six. He seemed older from just his life experience.

We are Family

Aaron's smile, ebullience and teddy-bear hug defy his upbringing, which was far from stable. He grew up with five brothers and two sisters, raised by a single mom and four different fathers. The fourth father, his birth father, was the only one involved with the family. They met when he was five years old, while his father was stationed in the armed forces in Germany.

From the age of eight on, Aaron was felt the desire to join the military, but he was not sure which branch. His high school had a delayed entry program for the Marines, so that influenced his enlistment at the age of seventeen. The Marine Corps then became his family for seven years, four years active duty in Iraq and Afghanistan, then another three as a reserve.

PTSD and Anxiety

After his stint in the military, the bad mental code of Posttraumatic Stress Disorder (PTSD) and the angst of isolation and self-confinement contributed to Aaron's spiraling depression. However, he combatted his condition aggressively with pro-active diligence. He used the relationship tool, seeking help from trusted friends, went to back to college to manage and leverage his future, joined a military support group in college, and hopped on his motorcycle for long bike rides, at times riding into the wee hours of the morning.

Unfortunately, his girlfriend, and mother of his ten-month-old son, did not understand his condition at all, a situation that pulled them apart. However, with a twinkle in his eye, he shares how his son taught him more than most anything else on earth and having a child was a true gift in his life. Aaron is determined his son will not face the precarious fate of his own siblings, who are currently all on drugs. His son will grow up having a devoted father who is involved and focused on healthy goals.

Win Life's Battle

Part of Aaron's current therapy is working out hard at the gym, releasing masses of good endorphins. He attends school, works and has his son three days a week and alternate weekends. Working out proves to be a better choice than lengthy bike rides with his busy schedule. After making the college baseball team, then getting cut, he also discovered softball, which has provided yet another extended family for him.

Aaron is creating a new life for himself and his son. He has climbed a slippery slope during much of his twenties, but fighting on the front lines has helped to build strength of character in his life. I have no doubt that if in danger, this young, loyal patriot would take a bullet for me; he's that kind of guy. A saying he picked up from the Marine Corps is, "Improvise, Adapt and Overcome." He knows that if he allows failure to overcome his life, he will have truly failed. This attitude has proved to be a valuable asset.

Aaron has developed good mental code to win life's battle. He is determined to complete his education. He says, "There's no room for error," and knows the biggest mistake he could make right now would be to lose sight of his goal. Despite all that Aaron has been through, I know he will cross the finish line.

Shifting Career Paths

Career paths in the twenties are a time of shifting tectonic plates, moved by the pursuit of education and interests. Many find it's not as easy as they expected to carve out a niche and future. Those who possess the right life tools will find it easier to weather the vicissitudes this decade brings.

Constructing a plan, even if it changes, will expand your possibilities especially if you develop your rare and valuable skills.

Aaron, currently in his twenties and Pat, formerly in his twenties, found that education and increased career capital could give them many more options for the future. Merely pursuing additional education or your passion won't increase your options and freedom. Constructing a plan, even if it changes, will expand your possibilities especially if you develop your rare and valuable skills.

 **TOOLS:**

Pat: *Management tool* to leverage future with education and development of skills; *Success tool* to identify future goals.

Aaron: *Management tool* to leverage future with education; *Relationship tool* to expand positive friendships and gain the support needed to face PTSD.

 MINDSETS:

• Commit to building career capital in addition to your education. It is not enough to merely build your life on a passionate dream. Career capital will help you fulfill your dream with rare and valuable skills.

• Surround yourself with loyal friends and solid support that will help you work through any obstacles and even stress.

• Learn from your failures and even the failures of others.

CHAPTER 27

EXPECTATIONS
IN THE THIRTIES

Tangled demands of education, family and career create a steep ramp with rising expectations, increasing pressure and stress.

Tangled demands of education, family and career create a steep ramp with rising expectations, increasing pressure and stress in the thirties. Lynda Weinman, founder of Lynda.com, was depressed on her thirtieth birthday because compared to what her friends had achieved, she felt she had not accomplished much. She felt everyone around her had life so much more together. Lynda started Lynda.com in 1995 when she was forty, as she didn't touch a computer until she was twenty-eight years old. She then sold Lynda.com, an online education company offering thousands of online video courses, to LinkedIn for 1.5 billion in 2015. Not bad.

As Lynda looks back on those years, she realizes her feelings were normal. She relates that many in their twenties and thirties are feeling the same way she did: comparing themselves to others, thinking they're not as good as they can be.[1] With idealistic expectations and self-doubt, it won't take long for the water on the stove to boil and overflow with increased stress.

Failed Entitlement

Just turning thirty at the time of this interview, Austin Carson was definitely one who compared himself to others and was feeling those demands. Many of his high school friends graduated just as he did, with parents who had steady jobs, guaranteed retirement and pension. That pink sparkle of a bright future was the way life worked, owing him a job and security, so he thought. He soon discovered otherwise.

Austin is already saying, "Getting older is crazy; you're naïve when you're young." Austin, who didn't like school and wasn't confident in his abilities, attempted several trajectories. First, he tried fire academy and paramedic work, then sold women's high-end shoes. Next, he thought police academy was the way to go: however, he wasn't in the best state of mind, being defensive, so twice he did not pass the psychological examination.

Personal Growth

It's understandable how disheartened Austin felt at this point. He realizes now how inept he was, crashing in the ripples and waves of stress, swimming toward nothingness. After his last failure, he was offered a job with the police reserves, with the potential of joining the department. However, he committed to working with a new start-up business selling home and auto insurance, mostly online.

Austin started using the management tool, leveraging his career capital by going through all the training and certification needed to sell with the new company. He also received a crash course in personal growth as he looked into the mirror of authenticity. About change he says, "You have to accept it, otherwise you'll be upset all the time." That is a personal philosophy he contemplates often to help to gauge his negative head trash, or negative self-talk.

You have to accept change, otherwise you'll be upset all the time.

Proficiency and Opportunity

With that personal gauge in place, Austin now realizes his past failures included Divine protection as it has pushed him to finish his education, expanding his future options and opportunities. Social media usually plays a substantial role in the lives of millennials, but Austin was candid about his thoughts; he has gotten rid of his Instagram account, as he found there are few people in the horde of constantly flaunted successes that are truly encouraging to him. With the extent of today's narcissistic promotion, flaunted achievements create a false gauge of comparison.

As a part of the entitlement generation, Austin had a rude awakening concerning his unrealistic expectations. He has calculated the value of a good education, with the realization that merely having a degree won't guarantee a position where he wants to be. Leveraging his career capital will happen with targeted education when proficiency and opportunity meet.

Leveraging career capital will happen with targeted education when proficiency and opportunity meet.

Didn't Want Her to Fail

Flunking seventh grade woke Diana Hansen up. She had been skating by, not doing her homework, subsequently she repeated a full year of middle school. That chapter in her life played a powerful role in determining the course of events that shaped Diana's future. At first, Diana never really struggled in school, neither did she excel. Having to re-take that full year of middle school was the turning point in her life and one of the main reasons she decided to pursue teaching full time as a career. It gave her the determination to take control of her future.

At eighteen upon graduation from high school, she announced she was going to college. She chose to use the power tool of a snaked chute to carve a new path away from the traditional Mexican family hierarchy of strong father and subservient mother. Her parents were apprehensive, not wanting Diana to fail again. Wouldn't a local trade school be better suited for her? No, not as far as Diana was concerned.

She was determined to go to college, even if she did fail. Diana chose a four-year state university about thirty minutes away from her family to achieve her goal. She made the additional decision not to accumilate college debt by living at home while working and attending college.

Broke the Pattern

Diana was the first and only one in her family not to only attend, but also to graduate from college. In fact, she didn't just stop with her bachelor's degree, but used the management tool to leverage her future as she finished her master's degree in education at age twenty-five. She is now thirty-four and has been teaching full time for eleven years.

Diana not only broke out of the traditional family cocoon of limited education, but also with the traditional type of relationship her parents had at home. She and her husband Keith, whom she met in high school at seventeen, share household responsibilities. She has learned to ask her husband to partner with her which is something her mother would never have done.

The two actually grew up together through those teen years and had to work hard to make adjustments, both personally and culturally. Diana even remembers Keith's mom scolding them both, as they were still just kids. Now Keith's mom is the beloved grandma to their three children. As Diana slowly moved away from the traditional Mexican culture of her family, the colors of their two separate backgrounds gradually melded, creating a whole new palate that is working well for them.

Time for Herself

Diana is like most moms of three young children, a six, five and one year old, as she has little time for herself with numerous demands from work and home. However, Diana doesn't feel the guilt many feel as first in their family to graduate from college. She has successfully paved a new way, working full time as well as raising a family.

Growing up, watching many families on T.V. sitcoms, she saw certain types of families she wanted to emulate and those she didn't. She gleaned insight from those shows in the 1990's, one being *Full House,* called the quintessential sappy family sitcom. This undoubtedly contributed to her determination and desire to complete her education and create a healthy family atmosphere as she saw the possibilities, even though the model was relayed through acting.

Failure for the entitlement generation can serve as a positive and helpful step in moving forward.

Both Austin and Diana, now in their thirties, faced failure in their lives that served as turning points. Diana faced hers early in the seventh grade, thus propelling her into action at a younger age than Austin. Failure for the entitlement generation can serve as a positive and helpful step in moving forward since failure is not a state of being but only a normal part of moving ahead. It's an important lesson to learn that failing does not make one a failure.

Failure is not a state of being but only a normal part of moving ahead.

Arthur Schopenhauer, the German philosopher said, "Mostly it is loss which teaches us about the worth of things."[2] That quote may serve as a mantra for many millennials who learn how to succeed mainly by failing. It takes an attitude of learning from mistakes, commitment to a focus on education along with career capital and perseverance, to push away the disruption and cycle of the bad mental code of entitlement.

 **TOOLS:**

Austin: *Management tool* to leverage career with additional education; *Personal tool* of a gauge to deal with head trash of negative self-talk; *Authentic tool* to see his honest reflection. **Diana:** *Refactoring tool* to identify a traditional mindset; *Management tool* to leverage career with education; *Power tool* of a snaked chute to change life direction and break tradition.

 MINDSETS:

• Face the fact that entitlement won't get you to where you want to be. Some don't learn this until later in life, if then.

• Understand the limitations of social media sites. Social media comparisons can be disheartening and discourage you with bad mental code.

• Evaluate the value of a degree, whether or not you have completed your education. A degree, combined with career capital, will eventually give you more freedom to pursue your passion as you discover what it truly is.

• Understand the value of change in your life. Failing does not make one a failure.

CHAPTER 28

FAST AND FURIOUS IN THE FORTIES

*When life provides difficult challenges, with resolution
and realistic objectives, the outcome may be
far greater than you planned.*

The forties hold high octane days with more activities than should
be allowed in a lifetime. This decade is not about illegal street racing
as portrayed in the American film franchise *Fast and Furious*,[1] but the
decade does carry many occasions of sprinting and dashing from
one activity to the next. Many have growing families and are also
building a career. These are hard-grinding years, with some climbing
up the business ladder and providing for uncertain futures, and
some trying to move to different locations for better schools and
opportunity. There are others just trying to make ends meet juggling
multiple family and work responsibilities.

A person in her forties may have already held several jobs, and
worked for different companies, possibly even in different fields. If
there are children, they are growing fast and are involved in a variety
of activities usually in multiple locations. It is a decade of managing
time, career and relationships with the years running by at a full
gallop.

Olympic Goals

Tage Peterson, who just turned forty-one at the time of our interview, had set out to be an Olympic athlete in the decathlon, an extremely difficult physical event that combines ten track and field events.

As the oldest of four siblings who all slept in the same room in a double-wide mobile home, Tage and his younger brother set out to carve a different future for themselves. They immediately got involved in sports, finding they were both quite proficient and naturally talented. Though a militant-style coach almost dissuaded him from ever going back to running track after his freshman year in high school, Tage discovered the decathlon the following year and used training as a shaping tool that would have impact on his life.

Planting a Dream

His sophomore coach in high school took time to train him and his brother, chiseling their abilities and planting a dream for Tage, "You can make it to the 1996 Olympic trials if you work hard at it." Both he and his brother trained relentlessly, breaking national records in the Junior Olympics and soon had a number of colleges calling, opening their doors for future education and training.

David Allen "Dave" Johnson,[2] who won the 1992 bronze Olympic medal in Barcelona, Spain, helped recruit Tage to Azusa Pacific University in Southern California, where they had a first class training facility and decathlon program. By his senior year in college, Tage had gained several *All American* honors, winning one championship after another. He was on record to at least match Dave Johnson's record, but the first meet of the outdoor season held its own unique challenge and disappointment. As he landed one of his jumps, his foot came down hard, causing a stress fracture. Two doctors said there was no way he could compete in the upcoming national championships, occurring six weeks later. However, he clung to the words of the third physician who said there might be a chance he could compete. It would take special water workouts and a strict diet program. He confirmed his goal and decision.

For the next six weeks, instead of leading, Tage was now trailing the pack with slow times that made him consider giving up completely. However, plowing through incredible pain, he went on, winning the national championship for the long jump and the decathlon. Of his achievement, Tage said, "This is something I almost threw away," after winning the MVP award. He learned that when life provides difficult challenges, with resolution and realistic objectives, the outcome may be far greater than planned. The valuable lessons in perseverance and dependence on his faith that Tage learned are still serving him well today.

His Last Jump

When a race is determined by one one-hundreth of a second, close doesn't count. When he started training for the 2000 Olympics, Tage's bone spur came back with a vengeance. It was 1999 and he was limping after just forty-five minutes of training, loading up on Ibuprofen. There was no way he could train the four to six hours a day it would take to be at the level he needed. When his doctor agreed to do the surgery a second time, he warned Tage that if there was a third operation, he may not be able to walk with his future kids. With that, Tage knew he had taken his last jump.

Tage's Olympic dream ended, but he has repurposed his abilities for another field, coaching young athletic teams, including his own son and daughter. "This day might be the last, so how do you want to spend it?" is his motto. Just as Tage has trained and pushed his body hard as an athlete, he will apply the same drive to many other areas of life.

This day might be the last, so how do you want to spend it?

Professional athletes have unique mental code challenges, as they are used to their bodies performing at optimum level. My own husband used to play baseball professionally and we speak about this quite often, as his daily routine now consists of multiple ice packs placed on knees and shoulders after his workouts. The careless stalker of aches and pains from an athletes' hard workouts remains a reality. With age, joints lose their suppleness. However, it is healthy mental code to keep the body moving, so I just keep our freezer full of ice packs.

Morning Reflection

I watch for Caryn Sawyer every morning, then wave as I pull out of our driveway. It's still dark, but Caryn is either running or walking up the steep hill outside our house. This is her routine seven days a week, an hour every morning, unless vacationing or sick.

Currently Caryn is walking by 4:40 A.M. I know many who would gasp at this schedule, but she looks at the hour she spends going up and down the hill as not only exercise, but her chance to spend time alone in private reflection and personal therapy. In the quiet, dark, she says, "I can talk to myself as much as I please!" One morning, she shared she was soon turning fifty, but she didn't seem upset. Since many are quite distraught with arriving at this half-century milestone, I set up an interview to examine the inner workings of her healthy mental code.

Laughs Things Off

Caryn feels tremendously fortunate as she loves her work. She has taught middle school since 2000, (bless her!) in a program that prepares students for college called AVID. (Advancement Via Individual Determination) Ninety-five percent of the students who continue in the program throughout high school are accepted into four year colleges, so she feels fortunate to head this program in her school.

Caryn was the first in her family to graduate from college and was never guided toward higher education throughout her high school years. She would have been a perfect candidate for the program she now leads, contributing to her passionate commitment to her work. A determining factor in her personal achievement was falling in with the right peer group as they helped shape her future outlook, like fine sandpaper.

Since Caryn is at least a quarter Sicilian, I was curious about her positive attitude and wondered what really boils beneath her surface. She readily admits to wearing her heart on her sleeve; however, she can chew on problems as much as she wants on her early morning walks with rants and vents. With a smile she added, "I just laugh things off." Her walks are serving to keep her pressure gauge at a good, healthy level.

Awareness and Gratitude

Caryn has a large group of friends, even former high school girlfriends ready to celebrate birthdays and getaways. Her attitudes of awareness and gratitude will help her through her coming decade with the positive tool of a blessed list and the authentic tool of a mirror of mindfulness. "Gratitude and gratefulness turn a negative into a positive," she says.

Those attitudes will serve her well as she continues expressing and discovering her own feelings on those lengthy early morning treks up a dark hill. I thought it was fun that Caryn has also made the mental resolution to drink less beer and more water, not even accepting a glass of wine during our interview. (She calls herself a "beer girl") Another recent choice for her was to eat raw vegetables at lunch, as she realized a pro-active approach and good daily routine are the best ways to combat future health risks. She is right, according to many nutritionists.

Tage and Caryn, even though at opposite ends of the forties decade, both focus on gratitude and awareness, positive and authentic tools. Tage, understanding the value built into his life by coaches and others who believed in him, now seeks to give back by coaching others. His life has been shaped and chiseled with training and guidance, physically and personally, making him the person he is today. His mission, or success tool, is to build into the lives of others.

Caryn, emphasizing positive tools in her classrooms, is grateful for how far she has come personally, now approaching her fifties. As her kids are getting older and more self sufficient, the personal demands on her time from her children are different than when the children were very young. This has left her with more time to spend with close friends. As the decade of the forties, leading to the fifties, can move as frantically as a swarm of bees, it is important to have those positive people in your life to meet the many changes of the following decades.

Deciding what not to do becomes more important than ever to give time to the important.

 **TOOLS:**

Tage: *Shaping tool* used especially through his athletic training, chiseling his attitudes and perseverance: *Success tool* as he gives so much of his time to others, defining his mission of giving back.

Caryn: *Positive tool* with laughter and a blessed list of gratitude; *Relationship tool* using her good friends to not only have fun, but as sandpaper to refine and help her in her coming decade; *Personal tool* of long walks up a hill to balance her pressure gauge.

 MINDSETS:

• Decide what not to do. It becomes more important than ever to give time to the important during the decade of the forties. "Your greatest danger is letting the urgent things crowd out the important."[3]

• Identify a place and time to talk through your thoughts. It will help you sort through your thoughts, ideas and feelings, even if it's in your car or on a long walk up a hill.

• Identify at least one way to give back. Giving back is a wonderful gauge of personal success and definition of a personal mission statement.

CHAPTER 29

UNTIMELY CHANGES OF THE FIFTIES

The fifties generates tremendous productivity but also bring unexpected physical challenges that can significantly affect subsequent decades.

The fifties are a time for change and transition for many. Children are either now completely out on their own, or getting close to flying solo. If a marriage is still together, many priorities have changed for each spouse. Differences in lifestyle and in life focus can strengthen or dissolve the relationship.

It's a decade where many parents begin "watching the journey" of their kids, and many relationships and even some friendships do not make the important emotional transitions. They go their separate ways, carving out a second act. It is a capsulized time of adjustment and hard work where many find themselves reinventing their lives as well as their careers. It can also be an exciting era of energy and focus with physical bodies that can still run and work hard without too many ailments. For many, the decade of the fifties generates tremendous productivity and output with a bounty of experience to be shared within an expansive network. However, it can also hold unexpected physical challenges which if not confronted can significantly affect subsequent decades.

Long Lost Family

Sitting across from Connie Pheiff at Starbucks, I knew she was in the midst of overcoming some very challenging physical obstacles in her fifties. However, I was also confident she'd conquer them with the same tenacity she has demonstrated with other surmountable hurdles in her life.

Connie shared that when she watched the T.V. show *Long Lost Family*,[1] the British award-winning T.V. series airing since 2011, she started crying because it brought back the flood of emotions that overwhelmed her when she first met her birth brother. Growing up, she knew she was the odd one out in the family that raised her. Nothing really connected for years as she felt like a foreigner in her own home. Connie was a lost, rejected little girl, who had three last names by the age of five and was sent to live with a family that was not her own. She did not know why, but a reiterating voice in her head kept blasting away, telling her that she was all alone--an outcast.

Connie barreled through her tumultuous twenties with a strong internal drive. Drugs, sex, and rock and roll were her gods. Married at nineteen, divorced, then married and divorced two more times, she finally took time to find herself. Alone and through counseling and support groups, Connie healed. Then, at thirty-six, Connie met Jeff. Two years later, they married and have been together ever since. Jeff has been one, if not the greatest gift, in Connie's life by loving her unconditionally. Connie and Jeff were as different as acid rock and the symphony, but they created harmony together.

Girl Scouts

Connie went on to become the CEO of *Girl Scouts, United Way* and Director at the United States Chamber of Commerce. Connie realized the importance of a good education with the leverage it would give her. With resolve she had built through the years, she went back to school and attained two masters degrees in business.

However, her world caved in once again when Connie lost her job at Girl Scouts. She decided to spend time with the man she knew as her father, who was dying of cancer. On his deathbed, he pushed her away again, calling her an outcast. Afterward, at age forty-eight, she discovered he wasn't her real father. When she began a downward spiral in depression and anger, Jeff handed her his credit card and said, "Go find your family." His urging demonstrated an act of unselfish, true love for her, something she had not experienced in her youth. It took two years, but after searching diligently, she found her complete birth family, including two brothers and a sister.

Faceless in the Mirror

Connie finally felt the weight and burden she had carried lift when she discovered the truth. She now had an anchor in life, no longer an outcast. Her birth father had died years before her search, but the puzzle pieces of her life finally fit together. Finding her family didn't guarantee a close relationship with them, but finding them settled the emotional confusion she had felt for so many years.

One day, she passed by a mirror, and she did a double take. There was literally nothing looking back at her. The metallic surface was blank. This didn't seem possible thermodynamically or physically as she felt she had finally found her true identity. At that instant, she finally asked the question, "Who am I really?"

Connie has now discovered the real woman inside her, different from the young girl lost at sea. Currently, she has one of the top-syndicated Internet radio shows in the country and is slated to be a host on the *C-Suite* series in New York.[2] Most importantly, Connie has learned how to love, not only from her husband, but when ultimately reconciling with the daughter and son she had from her first marriage.

The power tool of a patch can replace the mental code of shame and fear of the past to help individuals carve out their new future.

Her mantra of "Be Unstoppable," demonstrates the effect of the patch, inserting a powerful executable file in her life. It replaced the mental code of shame and fear of her past so she could help others carve out their new future. It has also helped her move past a "victim mentality," as she looks to the future, not the past. Connie has had to work through her own triggers of unresolved anger, bitterness and stress; however, she has gained further understanding of the reflection now looking back at her. With tears of love for her kids and a heartfelt devotion for her future work, Connie has found her authentic self.

Super Juice

It was a first for me; I had never conducted an interview with a person on a chemo pump, or "super juice" as Dr. Stephen Tracey calls it. At the time of our interview, he was between his sixth and seventh month in battling stage-four colon cancer. The end of the summer in 2015, we had received a letter from his office, announcing his condition. The letter ended with the optimistic phrase, "I got this!" I wanted to know if all that optimism was genuine healthy mental code or just a way to get through an incredible challenge.

All three of our sons had been patients of Dr. Tracey, a top orthodontist in our city. Every month when we entered his office, it was decorated in a way that spelled "fun," whether it was a life-sized Austin Powers, or a jungle scene, complete with giraffes and trees. Despite his illness, Dr. Tracey was still working regularly. I could tell by the number of patient pictures on his Facebook page with their "Tracey smiles." His future speaking engagements as an international lecturer and pioneer of many orthodontic applications were also listed on his website. It didn't look like he was slowing down, at least not much.

Change People's Lives

Dr. Tracey[3] has every reason to be depressed about his situation. At fifty-seven, he has competed in many Ironman triathlons, he swam from Alcatraz to San Francisco, trekked the jungles of the Amazon and climbed to the peak of Mt. Rainier. His mantra is "Live like you're living." He calls himself a really curious person and he related that his adventures were merely a way to step outside his comfort zone and to stretch himself. He also shared his success tool with a mission statement, which has stayed the same throughout the years, "To change people's lives."

He knew the power of a mission statement was not merely about creating a lifestyle, but also its ability to make an impact and a difference in people's lives. Braces became a vehicle for Dr. Tracey to give pep talks and guidance to students reclined in the chair, or cheer up a teary-eyed patient, offering them words of encouragement. He said, "The best part of my job is that someone's life will be different."

A mission statement is not merely about creating a lifestyle, but also its ability to make an impact and a difference in people's lives.

There were many unknowns at the time of our interview. For hours, he sits at the hospital with his constant companion, a bag dripping chemo medicine. He's hooked up for at least seventy-two hours every week. He works with it, talks with it and will not let it slow him down much, talking as fast as I do after several cups of coffee. He will not let the doctors tell him how long he has to live, as he feels that's negative mental code. He chooses to focus on the phrase "I can." He truly uses the positive tool of a blessed list.

Looking Forward

When I asked, "If you had the power to go back, would you?" He replied that he'd still choose to go through his cancer experience, for the numerous positive outcomes. It has brought his immediate family together, including his two daughters and four stepchildren. It has drawn him back to his roots spiritually, with a strong faith in God and the hereafter. He is not afraid of death, as he knows it'll be a win-win situation no matter the outcome. If he overcomes cancer, he gets to stay on earth with family and friends. If he doesn't, he knows he will be in a better place, a heaven above.

It was interesting that both individuals interviewed for this section of the book had unexpected and unsettling physical challenges. However, both are acting with vigilance and are continuing their lives because of it, which serves as an applicable principle of good healthy mental code. The "I Can" and "Unstoppable" approaches for both Dr. Tracey and Connie are pro-active lines of attack against extreme negativity and depression.

 ## TOOLS:

Connie: *Power tool,* a patch to change and replace her mental code of shame and fear; *Success tool,* her mission statement and branding; *Management tool* as she continued her education to leverage her career. *Authentic tool* as she now sees her true reflection.

Dr. Tracey: *Positive tool* with his blessed list; *Success tool* of a mission statement for his personal life and business; *Spirituality tool* to understand the importance of a relationship with a personal God, making him not afraid of what the future could hold.

 ## MINDSETS:

• Define your honest emotions, including shame and fear. They are genuine emotions that trigger a variety of actions, both good and bad. Doing so will help you to combat some of the negativity and self-focus those feelings and thoughts convey.

• Look in the mirror. If you can't see your true reflection, it's time to find what is holding you back.

• Treat the repetition of good habits and thoughts as your own "super juice" of a chemo pack to kill off negative self-talk.

• Take on a curious ,"I can" attitude. Thomas Edison, inventor of the light bulb, never stopped being curious. He continued inventing through his prolific life of eighty-four years.[4] "Be unstoppable!"

• If you are afraid of death, confront your fear with battery power, the spirituality tool to discover the condition of your soul so you can create a win-win situation in your life.

CHAPTER 30

BEGINNER'S MINDSET
OF THE SIXTIES

*A beginner's mindset, no matter what decade, is a healthy attitude
creating positive mental code and self talk.*

For many, turning sixty is rather daunting. These individuals have already seen friends or colleagues face a wave of health issues or even come to an earlier-than-planned death. Some shove aside the thought of retirement, facing uncertain financial times. Others activate serious thought about making a difference in the world or leaving a legacy for their children, considering the road ahead of them shorter than the road behind.

Whatever the case, facing the decade of the sixties with solid tools in place is pivotal in determining the next ten, twenty or even thirty years of life. How are you going to live in your sixties? Your positive outlook and beginner's mindset of learning and discovery will create good, healthy mental code, whereas giving up brings irritability, ignorance, and negativity that feeds bad, harmful mental code.

A Beginner's Mindset

At age sixty, Lynda Weinman sold Lynda.com to LinkedIn for 1.5 billion dollars. By this time, she had also authored sixteen books and numerous magazine articles. Upon the sale of her business that had grown to millions of subscribers, she said of her next step, "It's important to have a break and refresh and come to it with a beginner's mind, whatever that is."[1]

To be a beginner is to take on the attitude of learning a new skill, being an apprentice or student. Many reaching this decade of life have retired from a job, sold a business, faced a forced retirement, or made the decision to follow the route of an entrepreneur, by choice or necessity.

No matter how far you've traveled, what education, or people you know, there are more places to explore, truths to learn, and people to meet.

A beginner's mindset creates a strong foundation for developing and keeping good mental code, especially as you live through each of the subsequent decades of life. It helps you incorporate an attitude that includes lifelong learning and exploration. No matter how far you've traveled, what education, or people you know, there are more places to explore, truths to learn, and people to meet.

Willingness to Fail

Taking on the mindset of a beginner is not always easy, especially if you are just dipping your toe in entrepreneurism because self employment brings its share of isolation. To truly succeed takes the mindset of a constant learner, one who asks questions and sincerely listens to others. Assess your current position as your own professor of life, establish a workable plan, and create leverage for the upcoming years.

I would wager there are very few readers in their sixties willing to learn to skateboard for the first time, as skateboarding involves falling and getting hurt. However, if you can surpass the panic of a good tumble and focus on the fun, your new venture takes on a whole new focus. If you are willing to endure embarrassment or give yourself permission to look silly, you can clothe yourself with an assortment of bright bandages.

Attempting skateboarding is not that remote from starting a new business, taking a comedy improv class, writing a book or even learning an instrument.[2] My husband and I have decided to learn a new language together this year, either French or Spanish. My four years of Spanish I took decades ago are not only rusty, but also far from my recollection. I discovered this truth in my recent attempts to communicate to Spanish-speaking workers while they remodeled our bathrooms. To begin, we decided to establish our vision of fluently speaking a language. It actually sounds romantic to be speaking pillow-talk in French or to order a bottle of wine in Paris.

The reality of learning will hold times of laughter through our many missteps, speaking phrases that take on entirely new connotations with the twist of a phrase or pronunciation. The reality of taking on the beginner's mindset acknowledges the mistakes we might make. However, our language learning task will be easier when we decide to laugh at ourselves as we have permission to fail.

Derailed Failure

Larry Beck made a drastic U-turn in his life after looking back on years filled with feelings of failure and not living up to his potential. Now, at sixty-eight, he recounts times he was derailed. As I had dinner with him and his beautiful wife Janet, we sat at the campsite occupied by his thirty-six foot motorhome. He excitedly relayed his love of traveling and plans for their upcoming trips. This was quite different from the twenty-four year old Larry, who spent two years aimlessly traveling the country in a VW bus.

Growing up in one of the two Jewish families in their small town in Southern California, he woke one morning to find cruel and degrading insults scrawled in chalk on their front sidewalk. The sting of this hatred as viewed by a young child never left him and served as a basis for a lifetime of empathy for and insight into others. As the middle child of four brothers, he felt picked on by his siblings who called him the "favored son." However, he did not feel preferred to any degree, in a household he described as extremely dysfunctional.

Personal Toolkit

Even though Larry began as a straight-A student through his junior high years, he barely graduated high school. Unfortunately, he fell into a crowd that transformed into hoodlums at night. Strong peer pressure caused him to make some "fairly stupid" choices. Larry married at nineteen, but he had few options for a bright future. He took on the hippie lifestyle with no college education or job prospect in sight.

Some years later, after completing five years of college and working, he found that his people skills and his personal "toolkit" of natural strengths worked well for him. With his lofty hippy ideals and his ability to develop strong relationships, he climbed the corporate ladder for thirty-seven years with a company that believed in him. Now in retirement, Larry hasn't slowed down much. Maintaining healthy goals will serve as solid stepping stones for his future.

The benefit of healthy goals is verified with substantial research, as Yaakov Stern, Ph.D. and his colleagues found strong evidence for the decrease of dementia in those who remain actively engaged in life. The strongest leisure activities were reading, visiting friends or relatives, going to movies or restaurants and walking for pleasure. Maintaining intellectual and social engagement was also a factor as the activities act as a buffer[3] or cushion against the impact of aging.

Maintaining intellectual and social engagement acts as a buffer or cushion against the impact of aging.

Less Than Perfect

Both Larry and Janet successfully lost weight, seventy pounds between them at the time of our interview. Larry came from a family of diabetics and substance abuse and was determined to not reach the same fate as his parents and others. He was purposeful about changing the destructive pattern of his predecessors. When asked about his mindset and good code, Larry pondered and then replied, "I had to realize it was okay to be less than perfect."

Larry went for counseling two different times in his life, demonstrating a powerful constructive step toward healthy mental code. After the divorce from his first wife, he knew he had not faced many important issues while growing up. He had to confront those concerns as they were amplified by being alone. This was when he discovered it was fine not to be perfect and stopped being obsessive.

According to Larry, "Age is a challenge." I'm sure many who are facing the decades of the fifties, sixties, seventies, and beyond will agree heartily with his statement. Thriving, not just surviving is what most desire. Every day holds assessments, decisions and a resolution to focus on healthy self-talk. Each day also holds numerous choices in order to follow a healthy lifestyle with food, exercise and support of positive relationships. Larry is thankful for the positive relationship he has with his wife Janet, as he feels she has made him a better man.

Whether it's camping, biking or motorcycle riding, Larry sees these years as a time where he wants to enjoy every day to the fullest. He's outlived both his parents, so if he can reach his seventies and still be active, he'll be more than a happy camper.

Zest for Living

Pat O'Donnell, CEO of the Aspen Skiing Co., may not feel the same urgency as Larry does, but still, this director of a beautiful ski resort retired at sixty-eight so he and his wife could live in Grand Junction, Colorado, to continue pursing an active outdoor lifestyle.

Even though O'Donnell lived and worked in the enviable location of Aspen, Colorado, money and position never really mattered to him. He had gained enough experience, financial and career capital to make a transition. The move gave him time to do other things they wanted to do, unencumbered by daily job responsibilities.

The important concept to note here is that Pat had a list of adventures he and his wife wanted to do at retirement. He had positive goals and aspirations that created good mental code and a zest for living, taking him far into his retirement years.

A beginner's mindset encourages a constructive attitude and outlook, looking forward to opportunities, not backward at missed prospects.

Many who retire lose their zest and purpose for living. Lynda approached her years after Lynda.com with the enthusiasm of a lifelong learner with a beginner's mindset. Similarly, Larry and Pat still have places to visit, adventures to pursue, and roads to travel, whether hiking up the mountains of Colorado or trekking across the country in a motor home. Those objectives foster a forward motion and momentum with enthusiasm and gusto. Healthy mental code is created with goals, enthusiasm and a zest for living demonstrated with a beginner's mindset at any stage of life.

 **TOOLS:**

Larry: *Power tool* of the *snaked chute* to make a U-turn in his life; *Power tool* of the *patch* to rewrite his mental code when he went in for counseling; *Authentic tool* as he looked at his strengths to pursue a successful career.

Pat: *Management tool* as he pursued a good education, leveraging his career path to do the work he truly loved; *Success tool* with a strong mission statement of what was important in his life.

MINDSETS:

• Own a beginner's mindset. No matter what decade you are in, it is a healthy attitude that creates positive mental code and self talk. It encourages a constructive attitude and outlook, looking forward to opportunities, not backward at missed prospects.

• Identify and confront any unhealthy perfectionism as it breeds discontent and dissatisfaction. If you've not dealt with its harmful aspects, it's not too late to face that trait.

• Realize how important building your financial and career capital will be for you during the later decades if you are reading this and in your twenties, thirties or even forties.

• Never quit learning and growing with creative goals and objects that create forward momentum. Definitely don't be afraid to make a U-turn if needed.

• Decide to live each day to the fullest, even if you are not yet officially retired. Outliving the number of years of your parents creates an increased urgency to live each day to the fullest, similar to Larry. Pat's retiring at sixty-eight transpired from his personal mission statement, with his list of adventures to still accomplish.

CHAPTER 31

STEADY EROSION OF AGING IN THE SEVENTIES

With good relationships, you will gain support during the years of natural loss.

Sally Field, turning seventy in 2016, says, "Aging is this weird thing that happens. Even if your brain stays very young, your body just keeps going."[1] Sally is still actively starring in movies today, looking as great as ever with a healthy mindset. When a rock erodes, the surface is gradually worn away by the natural forces of water, wind or ice. Your body also has a natural attrition as you rub against the escalating years.

Papa, my grandfather, died in his seventies. I was the oldest grandchild of this wonderful man who had a mammoth sweet tooth, put sugar on his ice cream and called me his "little gal." My grandmother, Mimi, lived until she was ninety-six, twenty-some years past her husband. She continued to make mouth-watering chocolate meringue pies, crafted from rich bars of chocolate with one of the best meringues I've ever eaten, beaten by hand with a fork. She continued, that is, until she started to forget to turn off the burners on her stove. Nevertheless, she pursued life with good mental code and positive outlook during every one of those years, including the times when Papa ran for mayor of his small town. Part of the reason for her positive outlook and for his political victories was the support of friends and family, important at any stage of life, but especially as she managed the later years.

Celebrate Your Life!

My husband and I walked into a packed room of friends and family to celebrate Dick and Jan's fiftieth wedding anniversary. Dick Robertson had promised a fun time and great guacamole, and he did not disappoint us. On the guest list were many of his cycling friends. Dick's eyes lit up as he talked about cycling, in which he first started as a way to prolong his love of skiing.

Unfortunately, he had severely injured his right knee doing stunts, such as down hills ski-racing. So for him, cycling held the advantage of building up the muscles around the injured joint. Now, doctors laugh at him, asking him what he's done with his body because of the number of crashes he has taken. Dick has broken, twisted, or torn most of the bones and ligaments in his body. However, cycling has also played an important part in putting off symptoms of his rheumatoid arthritis. At that, doctors don't laugh, but shake their heads in amazement.

Math Whiz

Lest you think Dick does nothing but cycling, he also has a Ph.D. in mathematics and was a college professor for thirty-five years at Cal Poly Pomona University. Since he retired from that gig, he has been pursuing a different passion, still using mathematical formulas, equations and state-of-the-art computer software to analyze his wife's complex partial epileptic seizures.

Dick is purposeful about his study, pushing the envelope in a different way than most. He is fascinated by the theory, as he makes calculations and charts graphs related to the attacks. He hopes his configurations will lead him to predictions that can actually prevent future seizure attacks. In the past, he has been in contact with some of the top neurologists and epileptologists (experts in epileptic seizures), both in the U.S. and in Paris, but due to limited resources and diverse objectives, Dick has not made as much headway in his personal work as he had hoped for.

Lone Wolf

It would be nice if there were more people pursuing Dick's type of research to expedite the process and find some answers. Unfortunately, some of the exploration in his area has become a political issue, with other methods receiving the limited funds and support. It's a very narrow audience for his type of study, with possibly only two or three dozen people worldwide who have the ability and specific interest to really follow and understand his type of research. In that, he is truly a lone wolf.

However, just like the great composer Wolfgang Amadeus Mozart, who composed some of his best music in his later years, it's definitely not too late for Dick. His findings could very well make a huge difference for many. After all, Benjamin Franklin invented the bifocals at age seventy-six. In 1981, the wonderful actress Katherine Hepburn, at seventy-five, starred in On Golden Pond with seventy-six year old Henry Fonda. She received an Academy Award. In 1940, Grandma Moses, who started seriously painting in her seventies, staged her first solo show at age eighty. She then worked for another twenty years!

Good friends can counter discouragement over getting nowhere with research and negative self-talk by buoying you with hope.

Dick has friends who counter his discouragement over not gaining acceptance of his research and his ensuing negative self-talk by buoying him with hope. Then, of course, there's Jan. Dick loves his wife of over fifty years and yes, they have great friends who partied with them throughout the night with music and incredible guacamole. It's definitely not too late for Dick and hopefully someday his research will make a difference in the lives of many.

Certainly, it will be a celebration worth waiting for, guacamole or no guacamole!

Road Warrior

I first met Lynn Henish in my cycle class. I knew he was a serious rider, as he definitely looked the part with his full body suit and lean frame. I learned he is not only a biker but also a retired major airline pilot.

Lynn, now seventy-one, got his wings as a Naval aviator, only after significant times of crashing and burning. He barely made it through high school and flunked out of his first semester of junior college. Joining the Marines changed his life and going to flight school transformed his future. Lynn loved flying and was soon piloting large jets. He instructed young recruits for a full twenty years until he faced mandatory retirement at age sixty.

When Lynn felt a lump on his neck, he knew he needed to have it checked out but dread and fear crept in. Both his parents had died from cancer in their fifties and the constant phobia haunted him. In fact, he became so fearful, he turned to binge eating. Lynn added 100 pounds to his 5'7" frame. When the doctor determined the prognosis as stage-four throat cancer, his fears were realized. Lynn started immediate treatment to shrink the tumor before surgery. Also, when he finally faced his fear with the confirmed prognosis, the dread went away, along with the 100 pounds of excess weight. Today, he has been deemed cancer free.

Antidote to Fear

Now, Lynn is running hard. He cycles with those who ride fast, including many twenty to thirty year olds. He learned long ago that every lesson comes with a sacrifice, so he is striving to be as healthy as possible. He is even training for another marathon. After our interview, he shared with me a book of his well-crafted poetry, for he discovered writing also helps him further explore his thoughts and beliefs.

It is hard to know why Lynn escaped the sharp claws of chemo's destructiveness and cancer's finality. The doctor was actually amazed at his recovery. As a former high-performance jet pilot, Lynn isn't slowing down, similar to Dr. Tracey, the hopeful orthodontist. Lynn definitely confronts his days with the "I can" attitude. His mission statement and confrontation of the brevity of life will determine his own future win-win mental outlook in his coming decade.

The Color Purple

Nancy Graves was painting a mural on the side of her home in Hermosa Beach, California when I called. Her husband Tom washed out her paintbrush full of purple paint so we could talk. Nancy is a vibrant seventy-three-year-old and always appears to have some project or activity going. However, she is not too busy to educate herself and surround herself with support for her husband's recent diagnosis and symptoms of Alzheimer's.

Tom was my husband's high school baseball coach and they have kept in touch for many years. Alzheimer's runs in Tom's family with his mother and four out of five siblings having the disease. His older brother of eight years was diagnosed at fifty-three and died at fifty-seven. His younger brother is also suffering from Alzheimer's and is declining quickly. Tom, now at seventy-five, understands what could be a pendulum swing away. He is open about it, though not wanting to talk about it much or be a burden to anyone.

When visiting Tom and Nancy at their home in Missoula, Montana, I was struck by the organization of their home, especially their kitchen, as keeping an organized kitchen holds its challenges for me, personally. Nancy said she was always organized, but even more so now, as it helps Tom, having specific places to put items. They travel back and forth between Montana and California several times a year, and she has worked hard at making their small California residence just as systematized.

Take a Deep Breath

The flight from Los Angeles to Missoula is only a bit over two hours. I asked why they chose to drive the many more hours it takes when traveling to California. Of course—it was to bring Tigger, a beautiful eight-year-old golden retriever, who joined their family at just eight weeks. Nancy is hoping Tigger will live at least fourteen years, as he is a wonderful companion to Tom and her. One of Nancy's many activities is to be a part of the *Pet Partner Program*,[2] bringing Tigger to work as a therapy dog at senior centers, libraries, and other places.

There are days where Nancy says she takes a deep breath and reminds herself that Tom is not forgetting things on purpose. She knows there will be difficult times ahead, but she chooses to live in the present. They have been prudent about having their wills, directives and finances in order, updating all their records when Tom was first diagnosed with Mild Cognitive Disorder. So far, Tom has not progressed too rapidly, with just basic signs of mild forgetfulness.

Put the oxygen mask on yourself first so you can adequately give life-giving help to others.

To keep her good mental code intact, Nancy has not only researched her husband's condition,[3] but she also pursued her own counseling in cognitive behavior therapy. This has helped her with realistic expectations about what she can and cannot change. Like in an airline emergency where it's important to put the oxygen mask on yourself first, you need to pay attention to your own breath and health so you can adequately give life-giving help to others. Take a deep breath and remember that principle as one in three seniors face this disease at some point in their lifetimes.[4]

Potato Ukulele Trio

The Potato Ukulele Trio (P.U.T.s) is another one of Nancy's activities, performing mainly for senior events. She is intentional about relationships, with groups in both Missoula and Southern California. The oldest performing member of their potato friends is ninety, now in a wheelchair. Their favorite song is *Always Trust Your Cape.*[5] They even made their own capes, trimmed with pictures of potatoes. When you're in your seventies, you can get away with this!

Then, of course, there are Nancy's two reading groups, her hiking group and bridge group. All her friends realize that when Nancy can't leave Tom, activities will be held at her house, maintaining a wonderful support group for her. Nancy is taking care of herself emotionally with her multiple activities, attaining the counseling and support she needs. This is so important when acquiring the responsibility as full-time caregiver. This task can arrive quite suddenly and many are totally unprepared for it, leading to a spiral of negative mental code, confusion and discouragement.

Dick, Nancy and Lynn have realized the importance of a support group; Dick has surrounded himself with his cycling friends as well as contacts for his epilepsy research. Nancy has numerous groups as she cares for a spouse with Alzheimer's.

Lynn surrounds himself with his younger cycling friends. You may not have a packed room of friends or as many support groups as Nancy, but even a couple of key people who surround you with constructive encouragement and feedback will make all the difference in fighting off the dissuasion of negative self-talk. With good relationships, you will gain support during the years of natural loss.

 **TOOLS:**

Dick: *Success tool* with a strong mission statement to find a cure for seizures in his research; *Power tool* of a *patch*, not for his own mental code, but for the code of rewriting the mental code for his wife's seizures; *Relationship tool* contributing to encouragement for his research, buoying him with hope.

Lynn: *Power tool* of a *snaked chute* to turn his life around after failure. *Authentic tool* to face his fear of cancer with diagnosis and treatment.

Nancy: *Focus tool* to discard and sponge off unnecessary items to be more organized for Tom, facing Alzheimer's; *Relationship tool* with multiple circles of supportive relationships that are there for her now and will be in future years as she deals with the loneliness of a spouse with Alzheimer's.

 MINDSETS:

• Maintain a good support group of family and friends which is crucial during this decade. Don't be afraid to include younger members in your close circle, as they usually will add a fresh vibrant energy to your life.

• As well as friends, seek out support groups when facing health issues especially if you are becoming the caregiver for a friend or family member.

• Maintain some of your own interests and activities to receive your personal source of life-giving oxygen and refreshment, especially if you are acquiring the responsibility of caregiver.

• "Never, never, never give up!" said Winston Churchill.[6] Don't give up on your goals and aspirations, no matter what your age.

• Face the fact that this is a good decade to start scaling down with the focus tool. Discarding and organization become more important throughout the upcoming years.

CHAPTER 32

REASSESSING YOUR FUTURE IN THE EIGHTIES

An uncertain future will leave you isolated in fear or living every moment you can with as much energy as you can muster.

The decade of the eighties has its unique challenges. No makeup does quite what it's supposed to when faces have more creases than smooth areas to cover; every day is a potential bad hair day with fewer comb-over options; and your gait takes on the look of a cowboy wearing stiff chaps just dismounting a horse. Elizabeth Taylor says in *A Wreath of Roses*, "It is very strange that the years teach us patience—that the shorter our time, the greater our capacity for waiting."[1] Taylor died at seventy-nine, one step away from her eighties.

Physically, your body is moving more slowly, as if life is drying up. You know the train is traveling over the tracks with unhurried, yet intensifying momentum. The words aren't expended as quickly as they are disbursed in your mental thoughts. This is often the decade where the reality of an uncertain future will leave you with the choice of feeling isolated in fear or living every moment you can with as much energy as you can muster, one day at a time.

Winning the Lottery in Life

My friend Karen waved to a swimmer at the junior olympic-sized pool in our gym early one morning. Then she commented, "Maggie is such an inspiration. She is eighty-two years old." As I picked my jaw up off the floor, I watched Maggie swim another lap. Decidedly, I wanted to hear Maggie's story.

Maggie went to Shanghai, China for college right before Communism took over in 1949. She chronicles an amazing journey of meeting her husband, then a ten-year process of immigrating to the United States, a story that can fill many more pages than those contained in this book. That is her story to tell. Interestingly, but tragically, once they got to the U.S., they, like many other immigrants, had to start completely over, even with their education.

Her husband was a trained physicist, but had to repeat his coursework at California UCLA. Fortunately, with a U.S. degree, he was able to get a good job and support his family, which included two sons. They had truly won the lottery in life.

Working in your Eighties

Maggie, now eighty-four, still swims every day. In fact, she swims eighty laps every morning. She says it's her "job." Maggie also drives herself to the gym and arrives shortly after it opens at five A.M. There hasn't been a day when she hasn't greeted me with a smile or a wave. She says her daily swim also provides a place for her to meet new friends.

When we met for coffee, she explained she is taking a community college course in Japanese, studying the language an hour each morning after her swim. She is the oldest student in her class, unfazed by all the seventeen and eighteen year old students who surrounded her weekly. I smiled at the visual.

Regret it but Release it

Maggie's phrase, "For a moment I regret it, but then I release it," confirmed my opinion that she uses positive self-talk that results in good mental code. Maggie has gone through her share of extreme hardship, loneliness and fear. However, she has chosen to think positively, letting go of the irrelevant parts of her past to resist growing calloused. "The past is the past," as she says.

Maggie organizes her schedule and every day sets simple daily goals, starting with multiple laps in the pool, greeting a growing circle of friends, then educating herself in foreign language. Some of her former friends have a victim mentality, blaming government and others for their situations in life. However, Maggie is treasuring her current life and practicing good mental code with her attitude of thankfulness and gratitude.

Maggie looks toward the future, but like many facing their eighties and nineties with a relentless ticking clock, a good fall could rapidly change her quality of life. Caregivers, assisted living, health issues and loss of mobility are all real and certain challenges most would rather forestall or not face. Diana Athill at ninety-eight, writes about of her decision to move into a facility at the age of ninety in *Alive, Alive Oh!* "A sensible decision did not become less sensible when it finally led to the action decided on. I must accept that fact, calm down and get on with it."[2] I have no doubt that Maggie will conquer her future sensible decisions with stern resolution as she knows perseverance, yet keeps hoping to win the lottery. If she keeps that mindset, she will continue to win.

Walker Dance

I had the occasion to meet Sid Malbon, eighty-eight years young, in an assisted care facility in Bainbridge Island, Washington. Sid is the father and father-in-law of good friends Mark and Peggy Malbon and I was traveling with Peggy on a writing retreat. In recent years, Sid had outlived his wife after sixty anniversaries. I was curious to hear how he was adjusting as the years were now coming down on his head.

As Peggy and I entered the senior facility, we were greeted with a pianist playing "Beer Barrel Polka" on the lobby grand piano. Martha had a huge smile for us the entire time, as she tinkled the keys, never looking at her hands. I don't look at my hands much either while I play, but she was 100 years old and didn't miss a beat! As she played on, other residents started doing the walker-dance. I couldn't help but giggle—using a walker as a fox-trot partner was quite clever and so fun to watch! No one fell, which was also quite a relief.

Later, even with fingers cramped with arthritis, Helen played a beautiful piece by Chopin. She had turned ninety-five the day before and was working on a full program of just Chopin compositions. A Steinway grand piano graced her room. At this point, I started to wonder what they were putting in the water to have such lively aged residents. Was there truly a fountain of youth?

The Right Thing to Do

After Sid's wife passed away, he knew he needed help, so he moved into an assisted living facility. No one pushed him or convinced him. He seemed to think it was just the right thing to do after he looked honestly at his situation. Why, I asked?

Many people love to tell their stories, especially to a willing listener.

As soon as Sid started sharing his background, there was no turning on his favorite T.V. program. I found that he, like many others, love to tell their stories to a willing listener. I started to understand his mindset of good mental code.

At the age of eighteen, Sid contracted pulmonary tuberculosis and instead of going to the University of Wisconsin, he entered a sanatorium for two years. In fact it was longer than just a couple of years, as he suffered an additional attack. The best advice he received during that period was, "Don't fight it—do the best you can." So he applied those words throughout his life, particularly to areas he couldn't change.

After later receiving a full scholarship to finish his education, including a graduate degree, he, for many years, worked with the National Forest Service. Since he loved the outdoors, his hobby was working with wood. I admired several pieces of well-crafted and beautifully executed furniture he had built from scratch. He remarked, "Woodworking was a delight because wood did not talk back." Well said!

One Day at a Time

Sid does miss working with wood, but with the onset of a condition called "essential tremor," he no longer trusts himself with any tool. In fact, it's difficult for him to write or even type on a computer keyboard. However, that has not stopped him from using a computer or working on his files. He has a single remote control for lights, television and even his recliner in his small apartment and uses them often. I watched Sid cut his own food with a knife, refusing help to get out of a chair, and deliberately walk forward and backwards in his walker. These are all areas where Sid is doing the best he can, the principle he has carried throughout his life.

His family and a small circle of good friends helped Sid battle a bout of deep depression in 1996, as he lost interest in almost everything. His wife Helene was a mainstay through this time. He also received the medical help he needed. Now he lives one day at a time, realizing how limited his world has become with planned meals, daily movies, doctors, therapy and exercise.

The senior facility keeps Sid fairly busy and he appreciated our visits, but did not put any expectations on how much time we spent or when we would return. That made it a delight to sit and talk with him. Making the decision to move into a care facility is never an easy choice, with many transitioning out of a larger home carrying a lifetime of memories and belongings.

However, Sid is not a prisoner in his room. Still, he is creating small, yet significant memories with new friends who surround him during meals. In his controlled environment, Sid is experiencing shared stories and the sincere companionship of his new friends as they relive and expound on some of their favorite recollections. Athill writes in *Alive, Alive Oh!* that old-age friendships are slightly different than those made in the past. They now contain "Excursions into each other's pasts." They contain stories of "Lives still being lived, not for entertainment...brought forth only by warmth, sympathy and mutual esteem, as the material of friendship."[3]

A daily schedule of physical activity, mental activity and social activity is important at every stage of life.

Both Sid and Maggie are greeting each day with a schedule and routine. Their routines will change with unforeseen physical challenges, but they have chosen not to spend time depressed with the emptiness of solitude. A daily schedule of physical activity, mental activity and social activity is important at every stage of life, especially for those now in the boxcar speeding towards the centenarian years.

 **TOOLS:**

Maggie: *Positive tool* with her blessed list: "The past is the past;" *Success tool* as her yardstick of success lies in her swimming every day and continuing to grow through a language course; she is also leveraging her future as a lifelong learner; *Relationship tool* as she meets others swimming and in her language class.

Sid: *Personal tool* of a blessed list; *Success tool* as he works hard to keep moving; *Relationship tool* as he is making new friends; *Reflection tool* to get the medical help he needed when facing depression.

MINDSETS:

• Keep moving, even if it's difficult. Many are still able to drive throughout their eighties and longer, but be prudent when vision and response times are usually declining. There are many options for continued mobility and transportation.

• Be consistent with exercise. Exercise is your "job" and is not only a good mindset but is great for your overall health.

• Find some way to keep your mind active, whether in a class or other activity with other people. Even better is to hang around a younger crowd as they can learn so much from you and you, them!

• If it's time for assisted care, downscale enough to make the transition easier on yourself. There are many great options and if you're able, visit different facilities with a close friend or family member before it becomes absolutely necessary.

• Keep a schedule and routine as they are your friends. With a good routine, you will still have enough "brain space" to keep learning, keep growing and keep moving!

CHAPTER 33

FINAL CODE

As you shape, focus and continue to manage your life, don't forget what will matter most in the end- impacting others.

Final means the end. It is the concluding chapter, act or inning in a game. It is what is ahead for every person, yet getting there holds unique challenges, manifested differently for every person. With physical, relationship and career challenges, how you approach each decade will determine how you approach your final chapter of life, whenever that may be. For good mental code to overcome the bad mental code that threatens to sabotage your life, there are daily, hourly and even minute-by minute choices to make. The tools in this book, when applied, will give you the personal leverage and power to fight the onslaught of negative mental code. Here, I'd like to summarize some of my last personal thoughts.

A blessed list is important at every stage of life. We've looked at Aaron surviving and now thriving after Iraq, Afghanistan and even PTSD; Austin failing a number of times only to discover that his latest job prompted him to finish his education; then on to Dr. Tracey who wouldn't change his stage-four cancer prognosis because of all the good it's brought into his life. Looking for the positive doesn't discount the negative. However, if the negative wasn't there, the optimism wouldn't shine as bright, just as light wouldn't glow so brilliantly without the darkness.

Computer and Mental Code

It is fascinating how many life applications can be drawn from the virtual principle of code. The code of life is dynamic and ever changing, which is extremely powerful and should encourage you about your ability to change and create new habits.

I love to encourage others, although not just because it's written in my mission statement. Encouragement is my intention every time I play a requested song, write lyrics that will lift others up, craft a composition to be enjoyed and performed by others or write words in a book. That doesn't make writing and creating easy—I labor over legitimate sources to document statistics and the refinement of every section (or every piece of music) to make sure the message is clear and concise. In fact, it takes a huge thrust of energy and focus to finish well. When nearing completion, it's like being hours away from reaching the top of a mountain and all you want to do is take a nap.

I'm not sure why we remember some dreams and not others, like the dream I mentioned at the beginning of this book, but I feel like I was supposed to vividly recall that particular episode so I could share it here. Stories, whether fictional or real, bring concepts and truths to life in a relevant package.

In my heart, I'm a farm girl, as I love being outside, watering and pruning our fruit trees every weekend I'm home. My mother taught me to make jam and pies and to use resources wisely. I was born on a dairy farm in Georgia. Even though I didn't grow up there, I love seeing the roses my husband grows in our yard. He got the green thumb. So when I lined up interviews, I looked for the "genuine" and "authentic" in people with honest growth and principles, and I so appreciate how candidly people have shared their stories with me.

Simple Summaries

Decade of the twenties and thirties: career capital, failed entitlement. Many Millennials learn how to succeed by failing. It takes an attitude of learning from mistakes, commitment to focused education with career capital and perseverance to push away the disruption of bad mental code.

Decade of the forties: hard-grinding years with multiple responsibilities. The forties hold numerous days with more activities than should be allowed in a lifetime. Many have growing families and are also building a career. The management of schedules and goals is very important with a solid focus on important priorities.

Decade of the fifties: gratitude and awareness through life changes. Intellectual decisions will assist growth and maneuvering through this midpoint of life. There are unexpected encounters that can easily encourage unresolved anger, bitterness and stress, contributing to bad and destructive mental code bringing on fear and shame

Decade of the sixties: lifelong learner with a beginner's mindset. There are places to visit, adventures to pursue and roads to travel. Those objectives keep a forward focus with enthusiasm and motivation that lead to positive and healthy mental code. Attitude is pivotal in determining the next ten, twenty or even thirty years of life.

Decade of the seventies: importance of a support group. Your close circle of contacts are extremely important when facing such health issues such as Alzheimer's, or encouragement for work that has not yet found its significant place. You may not have a packed room of friends, but even a couple people who surround you with constructive encouragement can make all the difference in fighting off discouragement and negative self-talk.

Decade of the eighties: your world grows smaller. Routines are modified and changed with unseen physical challenges. Nevertheless, a daily routine of physical activity, mental activity and social activity is important at every stage of life, especially for those in the boxcar speeding towards the centenarian years. Commitment to some sort of physical activity is very important, both for the body and for the mind.

Overflowing with Celebration

There were so many cars, my husband and I had to park up the street for the memorial service. We entered the crowded room and secured our seats for what I was sure would be a moving memory of a life cut short. I gave myself permission to cry, packing multiple tissues in my bag. This was because I was not up front playing and singing, viewing the larger-than-life projection of an amazing and impactful life played out. This man was truly loved by others, as memorialized in his favorite quote, "A heart is not judged by how much you love; but by how much you are loved by others."[1]

Just five weeks before, I had interviewed Dr. Stephen Tracey as he talked for two full hours on my patio. He was getting better, so the doctors said. But his body could not hold up under the brutal ravages of cancer. The focus of the service in his memory was not all the inroads he had made as a top orthodontist or on his relentless adventuresome adventures, but on his humanity and faith.

> *"A heart is not judged by how much you love;*
> *but by how much you are loved by others."*

Dr. Tracey was honest about his faults and met them head on. Even as a forerunner in his field, he shared openly about his struggles and mistakes. This made him real, approachable and authentic. He was a lifelong learner and treated each adventure and challenge with gusto, even as I was able to take notes on what was probably his last interview.

I spoke with his wife soon after I heard of his passing. He told her of our interview several days before he left this world. He wanted to make sure she knew his story would be in this book and to contact me. I felt honored and had already decided to dedicate the book in his honor. Dr. Tracey was not afraid of death, as he communicated by his win-win attitude. Even though he'll be fervently missed, he is now pain-free in a better place, probably sky-diving through the heavenly clouds.

Live Your Unique Life

Every person is as different as a snowflake, with unique characteristics, appearance and emotions. Hopefully you have found and applied some important life principles and tools to empower you to change or alter mental code that is detrimental or destructive.

At any stage, if you wear the attitude of a lifelong learner with a beginner's mindset, that approach will carry you through most challenges with good, positive self-talk. Solid goals with even very small and consistent baby steps will keep you focused and on track, even into your eighties and beyond. You don't have to be working on a full program of Chopin as Helen from Bainbridge Island, but you will have your own exciting ventures that will inspire you, even as your world grows smaller.

Your Win-Win Forecast

None of us truly knows how long our physical clock will keep ticking. We can't predict the seeming disparity of survival from a stage-four cancer prognosis, as demonstrated between Dr. Tracey and Lynn Henish. Every person has to confront her own mental win-win forecast with her box of tools. No matter what decade you are in, my desire is that you continue to be a lifelong learner, greeting each day with a blessed list, laughter and the other tools, especially spirituality that will help you through life's changes and ultimate finality.

Memorial services are special times to reflect on the most important aspects of life. As you shape, focus, and manage your life, don't forget what will matter most in the end. Your life will have impact on others in some way. You can choose how. When all is done, what we give matters most. In the words of Charlotte the spider, as you help someone else, you lift up your own life in some way. Heaven knows we can all use a little of that. That is the good and healthy mental code I wish for you.

Ye Old Toolbox

TOOL	PURPOSE	APPLICATION
	Power Saw to cut a Snaked Chute to change the direction of your life.	
	Patch to write new code to exchange bad to good mental thoughts.	
	Scale to weigh your options in life.	
	Leverage bar in your life with education and expanded network.	
	Gauge to determine pressure and contents of your toolbox.	
	Screwdriver & Nuts and bolts of a blessed list and good laugh.	
	Hammer & Chisel to chip away at stubbornness and develop a thicker skin.	

©Deborah Johnson • GoalsForYourLife.com • DJWorksMusic.com

TOOL	PURPOSE	APPLICATION
	Trash bag to discard the things that clutter up your life.	
	Sponge to further discard and focus to see the beauty around you.	
	Magnifying glass to find any smelly code of thoughts that are stinking up your life.	
	Blueprint or plan to make changes and achieve goals.	
	Measuring tool to determine true success with a mission statement.	
	Sander/ sandpaper of relationships that are either toxic or beneficial.	
	Spiritual battery to determine your win-win situation in life. or death.	
	Mirror of reflection to determine your authentic and honest self.	

Decades of
Your Life

DECADE	MENTAL CHALLENGE	YOUR MINDSET Past•Present•Future
20'S	Career paths in the twenties are a time of shifting tectonic plates, with the many life changes that occur.	
30'S	Tangled demands of education, family and career create a steep ramp with rising expectations, increasing pressure and stress.	
40'S	When life provides difficult challenges, with resolution and realistic objectives, deciding what not to do, the outcome may be far greater than you planned.	

DECADE	MENTAL CHALLENGE	YOUR MINDSET Past•Present•Future
50'S	Tremendous productivity but also unexpected physical challenges that can significantly affect subsequent decades.	
60'S	A beginner's mindset, no matter what decade, is a healthy attitude creating positive mental code and self talk. subsequent decades.	
70'S	With good relationships, you will gain support during the years of natural loss.	
80'S	An uncertain future will leave you isolated in fear, or living every moment you can with as much energy as you can muster.	
	As you shape, focus and continue to manage your life, don't forget what will matter most in the end- impacting others.	

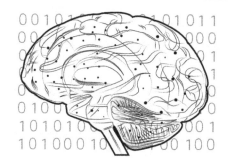

TWEETABLE MINDSETS
#BadCode • @DJWorksMusic

- #BadCode brings discontentment based on #shame and self-doubt, which is ultimately self destructive.
- #BadCode plays a role in your everyday life. How you define it, use it and limit it determines #yourfuture.
- To change #BadCode to good Mental Code, wake up to the fact you're being #sabotaged.
- You have a distinct #identity, or personal trade number, different than anyone else's. #BadCode.
- Your Internal Stamp is different than anyone else's giving you your own centrifugal #force. #BadCode.
- Reversing a #mindset can change simple #BadCode commands for your life.
- Mixture of hues is what happens when people #touch each other. Good Code vs. #BadCode.
- Too many shortcodes or #shortcuts in life leave you with wires that never meet and fire with #BadCode.
- Small revisions in your dynamic #mental code helps you modify and transform your life. #BadCode.
- The brain is like an #encryption device, hindering types of #BadCode.
- What looks perfectly fine on the outside can be #dangerous and destructive #BadCode on the inside.
- #Malware is like letting the mental worm of #BadCode in your life, creating chaos and destruction.
- #Change is inevitable-put protections in place to meet and accept change, for virtual and mental #BadCode.

• If a computer can be tricked into writing different data, your #mind can be tricked with faulty #BadCode commands.

• You can manage #risk as you perceptively weigh your options and leverage the outcome of #BadCode.

• Blowouts occur when there is unseen #stress not visible from the outside creating #BadCode.

• A Blessed List and #laughter are positive tools you should always keep in your Mental Toolbox to offset #BadCode.

• Diffusing an intense situation takes a clear focus and #ThickSkin to emphasize what truly matters, not #BadCode.

• For pithy and memorable, eliminate then concentrate on #extraordinary, preventing #BadCode.

• Smelly code is like mental #fungus that can stink up your life with #BadCode.

• A Yardstick of success will help you measure up to your imagined #expectations. #BadCode.

• Good #relationships give life and energy; toxic relationships kill your dreams. #BadCode.

• Read the fineprint in life or you may be in a Faustian #bargain, carried off to an unknown netherworld. #BadCode.

• Honest #reflection is a tool for positive change.#BadCode.

• For #healthy code with lasting results-reinforce segments in thousands of precise repetitions. #BadCode.

• #Malware of the mind lurks in every decade, entering your thoughts and brain to destroy healthy mental code. #BadCode.

• #Career paths in the 20's are like shifting tectonic plates with many changes. #BadCode.

• Decade of the thirties holds rising #expectations with increased pressure and stress. #BadCode.

• With challenges, resolution and realistic #objectives, the outcome may be greater than planned. #BadCode.

• A beginners #mindset is a healthy attitude, creating healthy self-talk. #BadCode.

• With good #relationships, you will gain support during years of natural loss. #BadCode.

• An uncertain future leaves you #isolated in fear, or living with energy. #BadCode

• As you shape, focus and manage your life, do what matters most to #impact others. #BadCode.

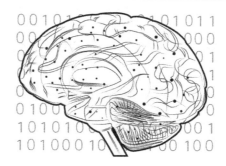

SUGGESTED READING
and LISTENING

Athill, Diana, *Alive, Alive Oh!*. New York: W.W. Norton & Company, 2015. *A delightful little book where Athill reminisces about part of her life, beginning in her grandparent's garden. I was wishing she could have included a diagram as her description was so graphic. It's a charming book, written by a woman now ninety-eight years old.*

Blanche, Wiesen Cook, *Eleanor Roosevelt, vol.1*. New York: Penguin Books, 1992. *This is an interesting biography, timeless in its appeal. It is not particularly a politically charged book, but one that covers the interesting life of Eleanor in a time where she forged ahead with a strong and resilient purpose.*

Brown, Brene, *Daring Greatly: How the Courage to Be Vulnerable Transforms the Way We Live, Love, Parent and Lead*. New York: Avery, 2015. *Brown is a Ph.D. who has taken on the deserved title, "shame researcher," with a mountain of interviews and candid reflection of her own life. I have re-read this book a number of times, owning the eBook as well as the paperback. Well-worth the investment.*

Conroy, Pat, *My Losing Season*. New York: Doubleday, 2002. (2003 Reprint edition is with Bantam books.) *This best seller is worth reading. It is all about family, love, loss, basketball--and life itself. I read this years ago and have the same opinion now as then-- it is inspiring and a book well-worth checking out.*

Cosper, Amy C., editor in chief, *Entrepreneur Magazine. This is one of my go-to monthly reads. There are interesting stories of challenges and success in all areas of business to glean and learn from.* Entrepreneur.com, @ AmyCCosper, @Entrepreneur.

Coyle, Daniel, *Talent Code*. New York: Bantam Books, 2009. *A wonderful book where best-selling author Coyle visits nine of the world's talent hotbeds to find the patterncommon to all of them. He found training, motivation and coaching are the key to developing true talent.*

Cussler, Clive, *Ghost Ship*. New York: Penguin, 2014. *This book provided some entertaining reading while I was researching this book. Little did I know this ficional novel would provide some reflective examples of our non-fiction cyberwar challenges. Easy and pleasurable reading.*

Johnson, Deborah, *Stuck is Not a Four-Letter Word: Seven Steps to Getting Unstuck*. Indiana: iUniverse, 2013. *Built on inspiring interviews, illustrations and stories to give you principles for moving forward in life.*

Johnson, Deborah, *Music for Kids*. Los Angeles: DJWorksMusic, 2015. *Music for Kids answers the "why" music education is so important, then the "how and when" to start a child in music lessons. It also makes a strong case for piano or keyboard instruction and its many benefits. Written in an easy-to-read dialogue between two moms, especially geared toward millennials.*

Grandin, Temple, *The Autistic Brain: Thinking Across the Spectrum*. New York: Houghton Miffin Harcourt, 2013. *This is an excellent book that explores Grandin's journey in dealing with her symptoms of high-functioning autism. With her Ph.D. and her ground-breaking research, she has made inroads in determining the habits and behavior of cattle.*

Hagerty, Barbara Bradley, *Life Reimagined: The Science, Art and Opportunity of Midlife*. New York: Riverhead Books, 2016. *This   book   has   a wealth of information about midlife, written by a former award-winning journalist and correspondent for NPR. She has done her homework with well-documented sources and takes us on her   own journey as a lifelong learner.*

Hamilton, Scott and Benet, Lorenzo, *Landing It: My Life On and Off the Ice*. New York: Kensington, 1999. *This is presently a bargain on Amazon. There is even an audio cassette available! It is an inspirational reads with good applicable principles from a gold medal Olympian.*

Healy, Mamie, editor in chief, *The Oprah Magazine* (Harlan, IA) *This has become one of my go-to magazines, not only for some of the articles, but for the book reviews, which are current and fairly interesting. I can imagine the fun Oprah has every month with her photo shoots, wearing new clothes and experiencing different surroundings for the theme. The graphics are wonderful and well-executed. TheOprahMag.com, @ oprahmagazine.*

Kendall, Jason and Judge, Lee, *Throwback: A Big-League Catcher Tells How the Game is Really Played*. New York: St.Martin's Griffin, 2015. *I learned more about the strategy and game of baseball from this book than attending multiple games. I was actually surprised how strategic the game can be. This is after being married to a former professional baseball pitcher for over thirty years!*

Klapper M.D., Dr. Robert, "Weekend Warrior," *ESPN Los Angeles*. Hosted on ESPN LA 710, the show is on Saturday mornings, 7-9AM, pacific time. *I call Dr.Clapper the "Vince Scully of orthopedics." He is a leader in minimally invasive surgical techniques and I catch his radio show whenever I can. You can also access past shows online. Interesting interviews and information.* http://espn.go.com/espnradio/losangeles/podcast/archive?id=6182844

Kondo, Marie, *The Life-Changing Magic of Tidying Up: The Japanese Art of Decluttering and Organizing*. Berkeley: Ten Speed Press, 2014. *I have read this inspiring book several times. I have yet to accomplish all Marie talks about in her book. In fact I barely got through one complete room. However, I will continue to follow some of the great principles she talks about to help simplify and see the beauty all around me.*

Laporte, Leo, *The Tech Guy*. *Leo's radio show is available nationwide in over 170 cities every weekend. I love all the tech information he provides from computers, cell phones, camcorders and cameras, gaming systems and home theatres. He appeals to the inner geek and has a great speaking voice as well.* http://techguylabs.com.

Limbaugh, Rush, *Rush Revere* series (2014) *Political beliefs aside, check out these children's books, not just for children! I have read two of the stories-- the adventures with Liberty, a talking horse who takes young and old patriots on time-travel adventures are delightful! I would suggest getting the hardbound, as I love good paper and these books have thick paper with wonderful illustrations in color. The historical facts are accurate and brought vividly to life.* RushRevere.com.

Simmons, Philip, *Learning to Fall: The Blessings of an Imperfect Life*. New York: Bantam Books, 2002. *This is short, butprovocative book that truly puts life in perspective. Simmons gave us a gift as he journaled during the days and years after his diagnosis of Lou Gehrig's disease. His positive attitude is inspirational and his words are well worth reading.*

Singer, P.W. and Friedman, Allan. *Cybersecurity and Cyberwar; What Everyone Needs to Know*. New York: Oxford, 2014. *This is a deeply informative resource book, written in an accessible style with engaging stories that a normal reader like myself can understand. It is current and helpful for both individuals and businesses.*

Twenge Ph.D., Dr. Jean, *Generation Me*. New York: Artia Books, 2014. *Twenge has done her research, profiling those born in the 80's and 90's as the "Entitlement Generation," or Millennials. Dr. Twenge uses data from 11 million respondents to reveal truths about this generation.*

White, E.B. *Charlotte's Web*. New York: Harper Collins, 1952. *After decades of not revisiting this book, I was surprised to find the writing succinct, descriptive and charming. I again fell in love with Charlotte as she worked so hard to save her pig friend, Wilbur. I was once again convinced how even children's books can captivate us with a great story and lesson.*

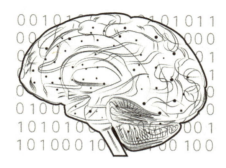

ENDNOTES
and PERMISSIONS

Introduction

[1]E.B. White, *Charlotte's Web* (New York: Harper Collins, 1952).

[2]White, *Charlotte's Web*, 164.

Chapter 1

[1]http://www.merriam-webster.com/dictionary/code.

[2]Jason Kendall and Lee Judge, *Throwback: A Big-League Catcher Tells How the Game is Really Played*, (New York: St.. Martin's Griffin, 2015).

[3]Saamah Abdallah, Juliet Michaelson, Sagar Shah, Laura Stoll and Nic Marks, "Happy Planet Index: 2012 Report," June 2012. http://www.happyplanetindex.org/countries/united-states-of-america/.

[4]John Helliwell, Richard Layard and Jeffrey Sachs, *World Happiness Report 2016, Update* (Vol . 1), New York: Sustainable Development Solutions Network. http://en.wikipedia.org/wiki/World_Happiness_Report.

[5]Interview with Guy Raz on NPR's *Weekend All Things Considered*, May 30,2010, http://www.npr.org/templates/story/story.php?storyId=127279055

[6]Look up: University of Pennsylvania's Authentic Happiness website, which has helped millions of people identify their strengths. https://www.authentichappiness.sas.upenn.edu/testcenter.

[7]Barbara Bradley Hagerty, *Life Reimagined: The Science, Art, and Opportunity of Midlife* (New York; Riverhead Books, 2016), p.56.

Chapter 2

[1]Gerald Wheeler, "Navy Destroyer Saved by Morse Code," January 8,2011.http://ezinearticles.com/?Navy-Destroyer-Saved-by-Morse-Code&id=5682769.

[2]https://www.youtube.com/watch?v=xsDk5_bktFo documentary on how Morse Code works.

[3]The Associated Press, "Symbol Added to Morse Code," February 17,2004. http://cjonline.com/stories/021704/pag_morsecode.shtml#.VyVnR7Ri7lI.

Chapter 3

[1]Benjamin Nelson, *Punched Cards to Bar Codes: A 200 Year Journey with Descriptions of over 260 Codes* (New Hampsire: Helmers, 1997).

[2]National Association of the Deaf, "Television Decoder Circuitry Act," https://nad.org/issues/civil-rights/television-decoder-circuitry-act This was an important Act to enable the deaf to watch television shows.

[3]"Estimated Number of Animal and Plant Species on Earth," The International Union for Conservation of Nature and Natural Resources, 20007. Fact Monster. http://www.factmonster.com/ipka/A0934288.html.

Chapter 4

[1]Albert H.C. Wong, Irving I. Gottesman and Arturas Petronis, "Phenotypic Differences in Genetically Identical Organisms: the Epigenetic Perspective," February 24, 2005. http://hmg.oxfordjournals.org/content/14/suppl_1/R11.full abstract by Dr. Azel Schumacher, 2005, Oxford University Press.

[2]Susan H. Babey, PhD, Joelle Wolstein, PhD, MPP, MA, Allison L. Diamant, MD, MSHS, Harold Goldstein, "Prediabetes in California: Nearly Half of California Adults on Path to Diabetes," March 10, 2016. http://healthpolicy.ucla.edu/publications/search/pages/detail.aspx?PubID=1472.

Chapter 5

[1]https://en.wikipedia.org/wiki/Binary_code .

[2]http://binarytranslator.com/what-is-binary/.

[3]YouTube-"Bad Code" song by Deborah Johnson: https://youtu.be/MSRhB1riKfU.

[4]Maslow, A.H. (1943). *Psychological Review* 50 (4) 370–96 - "A theory of human motivation". psychclassics.yorku.ca.

[5]Richard Goldstein, "Jack LaLanne, Founder of Modern Fitness Movement, Dies at 96," January 23, 2011. http://www.nytimes.com/2011/01/24/sports/24lalanne.html?_r=0.

Chapter 6

[1]Emily Upton, "Who Invented Braille?" November 26, 2013. http://www.todayifoundout.com/index.php/2013/11/history-braille/.

[2]Jean M. Twenge, Ph.D., *Generation Me*, (New York: Atria, 2014) 2-3.

[3]R.F. Baumeister and M.R. Leary, "The Need to Belong: Desire for Interpersonal Attachments as a Fundamental Human Motivation," Psychological Bulletin 117 (1995): 500.

[4]http://www.azlyrics.com/lyrics/bradpaisley/online.html.

[5]Julianne Holt-Lunstad, Timothy B. Smith, J.Bradley Layton, "Social Relationships and Mortality Risk: A Meta-analytic Review" July 27, 2010. http://journals.plos.org/plosmedicine/article?id=10.1371/journal.pmed.1000316.

[6]Mehrabian, A., & Ferris, S.R. (1967), Inference of attitudes from nonverbal communication in two channels. *Journal of Consulting Psychology*, 31, 248-252.

Chapter 7

[1]Andrew Ferguson, "A History of Computer Programming Languages," 2004. http://cs.brown.edu/~adf/programming_languages.html.

[2]Erin El Issa, "2015 American Household Credit Card Debt Study," 2015. http://www.nerdwallet.com/blog/credit-card-data/average-credit-card-debt-household/.

[3]Hagerty, *Life Reimagined*, 221.

Chapter 8

[1]http://CyberPro911.com.

[2]Daniel Coyle, *Talent Code* (New York: Bantam Books, 2009).

[3]Deborah Johnson, *Music for Kids*, (Upland: DJWorks, 2015), 75.

[4]Jack Lynch, "The Golden Age of Counterfeiting," Summer 2007. https://www.history.org/Foundation/journal/Summer07/counterfeit.cfm.

Chapter 9

[1]Grenda Gazzar, "Legal Experts to Weigh in on Porter Ranch Gas Leaks Claims at Town Hall Meeting," Los Angeles Daily News, January 31, 2016. http://www.dailynews.com/environment-and-nature/20160131/legal-experts-to-weigh-in-on-porter-ranch-gas-leak-claims-at-town-hall-meeting.

[2]Tim Hornyak, "Hack to Cost Sony $35 million in IT Repairs," *IDG News Service*, Februay 4, 2015. http://www.networkworld.com/article/2879814/data-center/sony-hack-cost-15-million-but-earnings-unaffected.html.

[3]www.corporate.target.com.

[4]Brian Krebs, "Target Hackers Broke in Via HVAC Company," February 2014. http://krebsonsecurity.com/2014/02/target-hackers-broke-in-via-hvac-company/.

[5]Terence L. Sadler, *Cybersecurity for Everyone: Securing your home or small business network* (Florida, Signalman Publishing, 2015), 52.

[6]Virginia Hughes, "Safecracking the Brain," October 24, 2013. http://nautil.us/issue/6/secret-codes/safecracking-the-brain.

[7]"The Imitation Game Film Synopsis," *The Telegraph,* October 2014. http://www.telegraph.co.uk/sponsored/culture/the-imitation-game/11158572/imitation-game-film-synopsis.html.

Chapter 10

[1]David Larter and Andrew Tilghman, "Pentagon: 10 U.S. Sailors Taken into Iranian Custody to be Returned," *Navy Times,* January 13, 2016. http://www.navytimes.com/story/military/2016/01/12/pentagon-2-us-navy-boats-held-iran-but-returned/78698018/.

[2]http://www.iusarecords.com/RecordsWorld.aspx.

[3]Kim Zetter, "Hacker Lexicon: What are Phishing and Spear Phishing?" *Wired,* April 7, 2015. http://www.wired.com/2015/04/hacker-lexicon-spear-phishing/.

Chapter 11

[1]P.W. Singer and Allan Friedman, *Cybersecurity and Cyberwar: What Everyone Needs to Know* (New York: Oxford, 2014), 61.

[2]http://www.wired.com/2015/04/hacker-lexicon-spear-phishing/.

[3]Singer and Friedman, *Cybersecurity*, 2.

[4]Singer and Friedman, *Cybersecurity*, 3.

[5]Clive Cussler, *Ghost Ship*, (New York: Penguin, 2014), 373.

[6]Deborah Johnson, *Stuck is Not a Four Letter Word: Seven Steps to Getting Unstuck* (Bloomington: iUniverse, 3013) http://www.amazon.com/Stuck-Not-Four-Letter-Word-Un-stuck/dp/1475996608/.

Chapter 12

[1]Nikolay Grebennikov, "Keyloggers: How They Work and How to Detect Them (Part 1)," Securelist, March 29, 2007. https://securelist.com/analysis/publications/36138/keyloggers-how-they-work-and-how-to-detect-them-part-1/.

[2]Garance Burke and Jonathan Fahey, "U.S. Power Grid Open to Attack," Daily Bulletin, sec. A, December 26, 2015.

[3]Singer and Friedman, Cybersecurity, 4.

Chapter 13

[1]Staff Report, "L.A. Hospital Paid 17K Ransom to Hackers of its Computer Network," *NBC Los Angeles*, February 17, 2016. http://www.nbclosangeles.com/news/local/Hollywood-Presbyterian-Paid-17K-Ransom-to-Hackers-369199031.html.

[2]Aaron M. Kessler, "Fiat Chrysler Issues Recall Over Hacking," *The New York Times*, sec. B, July 25, 2015.

[3]Andy Greenberg, "Hackers Remotely Kill a Jeep on the Highway—With Me in It," *Wired*, July 21, 2015. http://www.wired.com/2015/07/hackers-remotely-kill-jeep-highway/.

[4]Robert Moore, *Cybercrime: Investigating High Technology Computer Crime* (New York: Matthew Bender & Company, 2005), 258. For a smile, see the song "Hacker Crew" from *STILTZ The Musical*: http://StiltzTheMusical.com.

[5]Temple Grandin, "Behavioral Principles of Livestock Handling," 1989, 1-11. Reviewed by S.D. Musgrave and G.W. Thrasher. http://www.grandin.com/references/new.corral.html.

[6]Grandin, "Behavioral Principles," updated May 2012. http://grandin.com/behaviour/principles/moving.sorting.html.

[7]Ron Gill, PhD, Rick Machen, PhD, "Cattle Handling Pointers," Texas A & M Agrilife Extension. http://effectivestockmanship.com/PDFs/Cattle-Handling-Pointers.pdf.

Chapter 14

[1]Linda Banks-Santilli, "Guilt is One of the Biggest Struggles First-Generation College Students Face," *The Washington Post*, June 3, 2015. https://www.washingtonpost.com/posteverything/wp/2015/06/03/guilt-is-one-of-the-biggest-struggles-first-generation-college-students-face/.

[2]http://roadtripnation.com/leader/howard-schultz/new-interview.

[3]Galen and Craig at http://www.cyberpro911.com very successfully were able to completely fix my website. I recommend them highly!

[4]California State University, San Bernardino has one of the top cyber security programs in the U.S., with an undergraduate and graduate program. Dr. Tony Coulson, Ph.D. is one of the center directors. http://iasm.csusb.edu.

[5]Samantha Golkin, "A Good Defense is the Best Offense: How Early Detection Saves Lives," *Huffpost Women*, December 28, 2014. http://www.huffingtonpost.com/samantha-golkin/a-good-defense-is-the-best-offense_b_6057132.html.

[6]"Why do Diving Accidents Happen and How to Avoid Them?" August 25, 2015. https://www.bookyourdive.com/blog/2015/8/25/scuba-diving-accidents.

Chapter 15

[1]Brene Brown, *Daring Greatly: How the Courage to Be Vulnerable Transforms the Way We Live, Love, Parent and Lead* (New York, Avery, 2015), 60.

[2]*New American Standard Bible* (NASB) Version, Philippians 4:8.

Chapter 16

[1]http://www.brainyquote.com/quotes/quotes/a/aristotle145967.html.

[2]Philip Simmons, *Learning to Fall: The Blessings of an Imperfect Life* (New York,: Bantam Books, 2002), 23.

[3]*Readers Digest* (New York: Trusted Media Brands, Inc.) https://en.wikipedia.org/wiki/Trusted_Media_Brands,_Inc.

[4]Associated Press, "Cops: Suspect Stopped for Chicken and Biscuits After Heist," January 16, 2015. http://www.msn.com/en-us/news/offbeat/cops-suspect-stopped-for-chicken-and-biscuits-after-heist/ar-AA8dq7Y.

[5]Scott Hamilton and Lorenzo Benet, *Landing it: My Life On and Off the Ice* (New York: Kensington Books, 1999), 34.

[6]Grimm, Brothers, *Snow White and the Seven Dwarfs* (Traditional) https://en.wikipedia.org/wiki/Seven_Dwarfs#Happily_Ever_After.

Chapter 17

[1]http://www.nevworldwonders.com/2012/02/17-wonder-kailash-temple-in-ellora.html.

[2]Blanche Wiesen Cook, *Eleanor Roosevelt*, vol. 1 (New York: Penguin Books, 1992), 5-6.

[3]Brene Brown, *Daring Greatly* (New York, Avery, 2015), 56.

[4]Plato 427-347 B.C.

Chapter 18

[1]Marie Kondo, *The Life-Changing Magic of Tidying Up: The Japanese Art of Decluttering and Organizing* (Berkeley: Ten Speed Press, 2014), 42.

[2]http://www.brainyquote.com/quotes/quotes/h/hanshofman107805.html.

[3]Kondo, *Life-Changing*, 61.

[4]PRNewswire-USNewswire, "Jeaneology: ShopSmart Poll Finds Women Own 7 Pair of Jeans, Only Wear 4," *Shop Smart Magazine*, July 12, 2010. http://www.prnewswire.com/news-releases/jeaneology-shopsmart-poll-finds-women-own-7-pairs-of-jeans-only-wear-4-98274009.html.

[5]http://www.goodwill.org/faqs/.
[6]Elaine St. James, *Living the Simple Life* (N.Y.: Hyperion, Hachette Book Group, 1996), 13.
[7]Pam Gaber, "Gabriel's Angels: Pets Helping Kids," 2016. http://www.gabrielsangels.org/about_history.php.

Chapter 19

[1]https://en.wikipedia.org/wiki/Code_refactoring.
[2]https://en.wikipedia.org/wiki/Code_smell.
[3]http://tedxtalks.ted.com/video/My-philosophy-for-a-happy-life.

Chapter 20

[1]https://en.wikipedia.org/wiki/The_Beatles.
[2]Dawn Steele, *They Can Kill You...but They Can't Eat You* (N.Y.: Pocket Books, 1994), 280.
[3]Steele, *They Can Kill You*, 120.
[4]Rebecca Lake, Fear of Public Speaking Statistics and how to Overcome Glossophobia," April 28, 2015. https://www.creditdonkey.com/fear-of-public-speaking-statistics.html.
[5]http://www.toastmasters.org.

Chapter 21

[1]https://en.wikipedia.org/wiki/Cheers.
[2]https://en.wikipedia.org/wiki/Friends.
[3]https://en.wikipedia.org/wiki/The_Devil_Wears_Prada_(film).
[4]http://www.brainyquote.com/quotes/quotes/t/theodorero147887.html.

Chapter 22

[1]https://en.wikipedia.org/wiki/Burnt_(film).
[2]http://powerofpeaceproject.com.
[3]"7,500 Online Shoppers Unknowingly Sold Their Souls," *Technology-Fox News*, April 15, 2010. http://www.foxnews.com/tech/2010/04/15/online-shoppers-unknowingly-sold-souls.html.

Chapter 23

[1]Dr. Jean Twenge, PhD, *Generation Me* (New York: Atria Books, 2014).
[2]Beth Chee, "Today's Teens: More Materialistic, Less Willing to Work," *SDSU NewsCenter*, May 1, 2013. http://newcenter.sdsu.edu/sdsu_newscenter/news_story.aspx?sid=74179.
[3]Chip Espinoza and Mick Ukleja, *Managing the Millennials: Discover the Core Competencies for Managing Today's Workforce* (N.J.: Wiley, 2010), 14.
[4]"Muscle and Fitness Magazine," American fitness and bodybuilding magazine founded by Joe Weider, now published by American Media, Inc. based in Woodland Hills, CA.
[5]https://www.billyjoel.com/song/honesty-5/.
[6]Proverbs 27:17 says, "Iron sharpens iron, so one man sharpens another." It is estimated that Proverbs was written by King Solomon between the tenth and sixth century B.C.

Chapter 24

[1]Hamilton, *Landing It*, 155.

[2]Pat Conroy, *My Losing Season* (N.Y., Doubleday, 2002), 129. (Bantam Books-Reprint ed. 2003) [3]Conroy, *Losing Season*, 130.

[4]https://www.youtube.com/watch?v=s_MJg5zofOo.

[5]http://www.loni.usc.edu/about_loni/education/brain_trivia.php.

[6]R.T. Krampe and K.A. Ericsson, "Maintaining Excellence: Deliberate Practice and Elite Performance in Young and Older Pianists," Journal of Experimental Psychology: General 125, no. 4 (1996): 331.

[7]Newport, *So Good*, 85.

[8]http://espn.go.com/espnradio/losangeles/play?id=15309779 Bernstein's interview is approximately 40 minutes into the audio file.

Chapter 25

[1]D.M. Khoshaba and S.R. Maddi, "Early Experiences in Hardiness Development," *Consulting Psychology Journal: Practice and Research* 51, no.2 (1999): 106-16 is an interesting article on resilience.

Chapter 26

[1]Newport, *So Good*, 141-142.

[2]Julie Dunn, Aspen CEO ODonnell Retires," *The Denver Post*, November 13, 2006. http://www.denverpost.com/ci_4653724.

Chapter 27

[1]http://roadtripnation.com/leader/lynda-weinman/interview.

[2]https://www.goodreads.com/author/quotes/11682.Arthur_ Schopenhauer from Arthur Schopenhauer, *Parerga and Paralipomena* (United Kingdom, Clarendon Press, 2001) German philosopher (1788-1860).

Chapter 28

[1]Fast and Furious, distributed by Universal Pictures, was established with the 2001 film, The Fast and the Furious, followed by six sequels to this date. As of May 2015, it was Universal's biggest franchise of all time. David Gonzales (April 6, 2015). "'Furious 7' Marks Universal's Biggest Franchise Ever". *Forbes*. Retrieved May 2015.

[2]https://en.wikipedia.org/wiki/Dave_Johnson_(decathlete).

[3]Charles Hummel, *Tyrany of the Urgent* (Illinois, IVP Books, 1994), 5.

Chapter 29

[1]https://en.wikipedia.org/wiki/Long_Lost_Family.

[2]http://c-suitenetwork.com.

[3]http://www.traceyortho.com/default.aspx.

[4]Carol S. Dweck, Ph.D. *Mindset: The new Psychology of Success* (N.Y.: Ballantine Books, 2006), 56.

Chapter 30

[1]Emily Inverso, "Lynda Weinman Announces Exit as Executive Chair of Lynda.com," *Forbes*, June 10, 2015. http://www.forbes.com/sites/ emilyinverso/2015/06/10/lynda-weinman-announces-exit-as-executive-chair-of-lynda-com/#4c2b3e9b389b.

²See http://DJWorksMusic.com/learn-piano-online/ for piano courses. Great for those who used to play and want to play again!

³N. Scarmeas, G. Levy, M.X. Tang and Y. Stern, "Influence of Leisure Activity on the Incidence of Alzheimer's Disease," *Neurology* 57, no. 12 (2001), 2236-42.

Chapter 31

¹Sally Field, People Magazine (March 21, 2016), 84.

²https://petpartners.org.

³Nancy L. Mace,M.A. and Peter V. Rabins, M.D., M.PH. *The 36-Hour Day: A Family Guide to Caring for People who have Alzheimer's Disease*, Fifth Edition (New York: Warner Books, 2011).

⁴http://www.alz.org/facts/.

⁵Nancy's favorite version of Always Trust Your Cape is this one: https://youtu.be/j4q-Q6LSfuI.

⁶http://www.brainyquote.com/quotes/quotes/w/winstonchu143691.html.

Chapter 32

¹https://www.goodreads.com/work/quotes/1165965-a-wreath-of-roses.

²Diana Athill, *Alive, Alive Oh!* (New York: Norton, 2016) 104.

³Athill, *Alive*, 112.

Chapter 33

¹Quote by L. Frank Baum in *The Wonderful World of Oz*.

Permissions *(in order of appearance)*

Robin Freeland, interviewed by author.

Dr. Tony Coulson, Ph.D., interviewed by author.

Aaron Copas, interviewed by author.

Austin Carson, interviewed by author.

Diana Hansen, interviewed by author.

Tage Peterson, interviewed by author.

Caryn Sawyer, interviewed by author.

Connie Pheiff, interviewed by author. www.UporOut.com

Dr. Stephen Tracey, interviewed by author.

Larry Beck, interviewed by author.

Dick Robertson, interviewed by author.

Lynn Henish, interviewed by author.

Nancy Graves, interviewed by author.

Maggie (last name ommitted by request), interviewed by author.

Sid Malbon, interviewed by author.

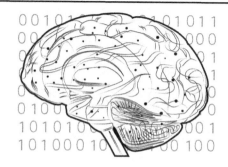

INDEX

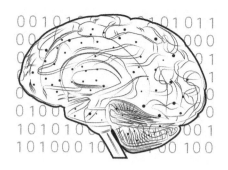

About Deborah

Deborah Johnson is an award-winning national recording artist, composer, author and educator. Her ability to relate to a multi-generational audience doesn't merely come from her Master's Degree, but also from her natural abilities and varied experience. She has not only written three full-length staged musicals, but successfully produced two world premieres, working with a varied cast of characters and temperaments. She has also successfully hosted and coordinated artist showcase rooms all across the country in national booking conferences, working on both sides of the fence, with agents and artist teams.

With over two dozen albums, four books and hundreds of songs, Deborah understands how to complete projects successfully. She also understands the challenges of change in todays economic climate and the healthy mental code that is necessary to do so. She is passionate about her work, displayed by the volume of her output and research.

As an entertainer, she has toured the world and has been up for a number of Grammy Awards. Deborah has performed large stage concerts with Double Grandé, a dueling piano (but different!) headliner act, also incorporating multi-media and her soaring vocals. Give her a microphone and keyboard and you will experience her deft ability to move between an impactful message and music. There are only a handful of women in the world with her abilities, and only one with her heart and smile: Deborah Johnson.